D1498720

Dominated Man

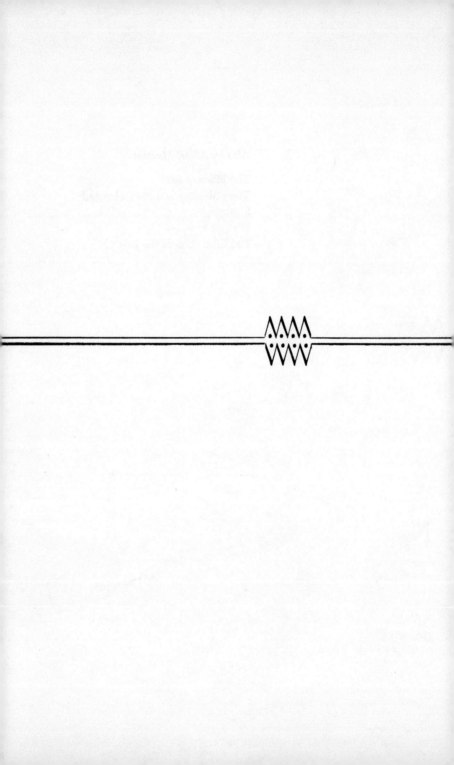

ALBERT MEMMI

DOMINATED MAN

Notes towards a Portrait

Orion Press • *New York*

First printing
All rights reserved
© *1968, by Albert Memmi*
Library of Congress Catalogue Card Number: 68–30771
Manufactured in the United States of America

"I considered all the oppressions that
are done under the sun."   *Ecclesiastes*

"The poor are the Negroes of Europe."   *Chamfort*

"Women are the proletarians of man."   *Marx*

"I think of the African problem; only a Jew
can understand it in its full profundity."   *Theodor Herzl*

Preface

Sketches for a Portrait of Dominated Man

I had promised myself not to undertake a general portrait of the oppressed until I had understood the majority of contemporary oppressed peoples; undoubtedly a large number remain to be heard.

Thus, this book is merely a first attempt; I shall have to return to the problem at a later time. These various studies are the first steps towards a major book on oppression, which I am always planning, which I might never achieve, but towards which I advance every day.

I do feel, nonetheless, that this collection of different experiences could at this point suggest, beyond the specific nature of each, a first portrait sketch of the dominated man of our time.

Furthermore, if all of these essays in this collection were written under precise circumstances, they were still written with one single intention: to contribute, by means of a partial sketch, to the completion of this future portrait.

In reading these, the reader will discover in addition some of the tools, concepts and hypotheses which have served me for one or another particular subject: the counter-myth as concerns the American black, woman's self-rejection, the notion of deficiency apropos the colonized.

The reader should not be surprised to find that I dedicate such a large place to the part played by racism, in a collection built on the various figures of the oppressed. Racism is, I believe, the symbol and the sum of all oppression.

Contents

V. The Woman

VI. The Domestic Servant

RACISM AND OPPRESSION

I

THE
BLACK
MAN

(Introduction to the French edition of
The Negro Protest, Editions Maspero, 1965.)

1

The Paths of the Revolt

In May, 1963, a Boston television station invited three famous black leaders to come and explain the meaning of the black revolt. Each of them gave his own interpretation and offered his solution to one of the most frightening crises that threatens the United States.[1] I do not know in what order they actually arrived at the studio; remarkably enough, though, the interviewer, and later the publisher, chose to present their speeches in the following sequence: James Baldwin, Malcolm X, Martin Luther King. There is a reason, too, for this order of presentation, in particular for placing King at the end: clearly it is he who is the favorite of American television, which hopes that his arguments win the day. But objectively this sequence is

---

[1] I was finishing this introductory text when the news arrived of the assassination of Malcolm X. It will very surely be said that he had preached violence too often not to fall a victim to it himself. But why *did* he resort to violence? The violence of the oppressed is a mere reflection of the violence of the oppressor. By his death Malcolm X is not signing an admission of error or defeat, but confirming, unhappily, that oppression is an infernal machine, and that from the bond between oppressor and oppressed there is no escape.

THE BLACK MAN

wrong. History has taught us, in many a hard lesson, that *in revolt there is a certain rhythm*. It is this: King, or Baldwin, but Malcolm X certainly last.

I have only met one of these three men—Baldwin—but I have no difficulty in imagining the others. Colonization has shown me these *types* of suffering humanity by the score. King is the moderate, who knows how to allay the fears of his adversary, how to restrain the impatience of his troops, and how to win himself allies: in fact, he is already a politician, a future head of state maybe, to whom the role of leader will at first be entrusted, but who will not remain in that position, his being an interim office.

Baldwin is the intellectual, sincere and emotional, or, in other words, intelligent, passionate and tormented; understanding everything and forgiving much; with friends in the enemy camp—one who could not abandon his friends or those he loves, but who knows that his friendships and his loves are already doomed, already impossible ones. For he has also grasped the fact that the moderates are by now in the wrong, that the time for moderation and understanding is past, and that these qualities have been engulfed in the rising tide of violence, for which dreadful preparations are being made on both sides.

This violence is personified by Malcolm X. For him, it's all over; Malcolm no longer understands anyone, nor wishes to understand anyone. He has no friends on the other side and perhaps never has had; in any case, he would not allow himself such ties, because for him the battle has already begun, overriding all other considerations, and it is not right to compromise with the enemy. This man of violence accuses, condemns and excludes even more virulently certain members of his own race, for a black man who does not fight with all his strength is worse than an enemy: he is a traitor, a vile, noxious individual, more dangerous than the enemy outside the ranks, because he is underhanded and deceitful. Malcolm and King seem totally

opposed, and at an impossible distance from one another. It is
obvious that King would rather avoid mentioning Malcolm; he
might lose his patience and forget his love of humanity. Malcolm does not mince matters: "King is the best weapon the
Whites have ever had . . ."

And yet King, Baldwin and Malcolm X do not represent
three different historical solutions to the black problem, three
possible choices for the Americans. We do not find a variety of
physiognomies among the oppressed: one, as it were, the winning look of the good friend and companion; another the face
of the cultured intellectual, ready to negotiate, against all odds,
and still fervently hoping to win conviction; the third, the
desperate expression of one who no longer has faith in anything but war. No, there is only one face, undergoing a gradual
change of expression, from pained surprise, still full of hope, to
hatred and violence, to the desire for destruction and death.
King, Baldwin and Malcolm X are signposts along the same
inexorable road of revolt; once men have started on that journey it is rare for them not to go right on to the end.

Without a doubt, King is the most noble figure among them,
the least disturbing, so to speak: "Love your oppressors as
yourselves," he says, or almost. And he only adds the "or almost" because this unnatural love so shocks his own followers.
Read the fine distinctions he draws between the different kinds
of love. This is not merely a subtle and ingenious mental exercise; it is, I believe, the outward sign of something to be found
deep within every oppressed creature. For the oppressed are
not filled solely with resentment against their oppressors; they
also admire them and would even actually love them, with a
kind of love, if they could.

From the point of view of mental hygiene, King's solution is
perhaps healthier and more restful for everyone, including the
oppressed. King is advocating a kind of collective Yoga, a lesson in relaxation and self-control, that is not unattractive. To be
able to stay calm, and to relax mentally, even when insulted,

even under blows, demands a certain degree of courage. King is certainly not lacking in this quality: fourteen times he has been to prison, and he is always ready to re-begin his non-violent demonstrations, which in fact rarely end without entailing some violence, directed solely against the blacks.

Only, says Baldwin, even now no one listens any longer to this admirable man; no one, whether black or white. If he still retains a certain moral ascendancy over the South, he no longer has any authority in the North. King has assuredly spared America much bloodshed, for which he was justly awarded the Nobel Peace Prize. He has certainly done much to preserve the unity of the American nation; but, must we continue to cling to this unity? Is it really relevant from now on for black Americans? Loving one's enemy, asserts King, and refusing to fight back is far more effective than hatred and revolutionary violence. But, given a certain degree of oppression, it is possible that this does not necessarily still hold good. We know how the memory of Gandhi lives in the imagination of many; it is understandable that revolutionary chiefs should at some point be tempted by such an apparently economical procedure as a non-violent revolution. But there is one all-important difference between King's situation and Gandhi's: in India, there were countless Indians to a handful of English; in this case, there are 20 million blacks in a population of 200 million whites, who at least contribute to their misery. All the Indians had to do was to lie down in order to cover the surface of the earth, and drown their oppressors in a human tide. The trains were brought to a standstill, so we are told, halted by the bodies of men lying on the rails. The blacks are one to ten, not counting the dogs; they are members of that most vulnerable category of oppressed humanity, whose misfortune is aggravated by isolation in a minority group. If we need proof of this it may be found in the fact that the demonstrations organized by King on the whole only succeeded where the blacks were relatively numerous.

The Paths of the Revolt

In contrast to King, with his prestige (he is black, but an acknowledged sovereign), his humanity (he is a preacher), his culture (he is a doctor of theology), his good breeding, his diplomacy, his self-control and his courtesy, Malcolm cuts a sinister figure. Possibly he really is sinister. A man who neither smokes nor drinks, who avoids women and seems so coldly hostile, so passionately calculating, so concentrated on a single aim to the exclusion of all else—such a creature is scarcely to be endured. He is certainly determined to do his worst and will probably stop at nothing; he rejoiced in public over the assassination of Kennedy (that reminded me of the monstrous jubilation of a colonized friend at the news of the terrible floods in Holland that killed so many people: he saw in these victims only the ghosts of his former colonial oppressors). In short, Malcolm is hateful to others and very probably to himself as well.

Dreadful though it may seem, the truth is that the revolutionary is a far from attractive figure; and he becomes progressively more objectionable the more he acquiesces in his revolt. He acquires ugly traits and idiosyncrasies, the symptoms of the poison of anger and shame he feels within himself, that are henceforth impossible to restrain. A few years ago, after I had published *The Colonizer and the Colonized,* I was asked why I had not also drawn the portrait of the decolonized. I did not like the question: it sounded to me like a trick. I assumed it implied: "Look how they have turned out, your former colonial subjects that you took such trouble to defend! Look how they are using the freedom they made such a fuss about: confusion and hatred, racism in reverse—a nice mess!" The Congo was a godsend for such charitable souls: decolonization sweeping away the old colonial order without managing to impose its own quite quickly enough. It is true that the revolutionary wears a more frightening aspect than the oppressed who is still apparently on good terms with his oppressor. The black who turns revolutionary is certainly less likeable, in a manner of

THE BLACK MAN

speaking, than the Good Negro, the shoe-shine boy or gentle-
man's lackey, even when the latter decides to demonstrate,
under the tutelage of King.

However, people must be brought to understand at last that
these two are one and the same person; part of the same revolutionary force caught at different moments of its career. I did
not draw a separate portrait of decolonized man, because, after
all, it seemed quite obvious to me that it was the same, with the
exception of a few minor features, as that of colonized man.
The decolonized races were simply bringing the revolt to a
close, finishing it off, as it were. Though this is too often overlooked, a decolonized nation is actually only a nation undergoing the process of decolonization, and still defining itself with
reference to colonization. Most of its often highly ambiguous
dealings with Europeans might be explained thus: its revolt is
not yet quite over and done with; for this reason its resentment
against them still smoulders, while its former admiration for
them is being rekindled.[1]

In the same way, the parts played by King and Malcolm X
are not from an historical point of view mutually exclusive, or
contradictory: the one is called forth by the other, follows on
from it and rounds it off. King is the victim of oppression who
still exercises self-restraint, because he still believes in the possibility of negotiation. If we want to negotiate, we must inspire
confidence, not make exorbitant demands at the outset, nor
scare the enemy away, even by the revelation of miseries that
might be too repellent to him. On the day set aside for negotiation, we must put on our Sunday best, and not explode in anger
before the enemy, not even make a show of our humiliation.
Deeper down still, King is the victim of oppression who per-
sists in wanting to resemble his oppressor. The oppressor will always be his model. But here, probably, is the decisive stage in
the journey, the turning point on which depends the definitive

[1] As a matter of fact, I did deal briefly with all this in a few pages at
the end of *The Colonizer and the Colonized.*

orientation of the revolutionary's destiny: Malcolm furiously rejects all similarity with the white man. He has taken his leave, given notice to his master, whom from now on he execrates.

It is clear, then, that at this point a new and fascinating chapter opens in the history of oppression. From here on the oppressed want to forge ahead by themselves, to find their own peculiar and individual path, entirely cut off from their former overlords, and at first in direct opposition to them; from now on they will acquiesce in the ugliness of their own reactions, which they will no longer attempt to disguise; instead they will make use of them, inducing in themselves hideous paroxysms of hate. They will in fact be accepting their own negative condition. But at the same time, since isolation is hard, they will not be turning inward to find in themselves the necessary strength to bear it. They will persuade themselves, for instance, of the boundless grandeur of their past and of the values of their race, convinced that they need only return to that source to find there all the human qualities they need to help them live and fight. In short, whereas King's whole philosophy can be summed up in the word integration, Malcolm is already working towards independence.

And yet, I repeat, there is no definite rift between these two men, no novelty in the one independent of the other. Baldwin who is so much closer to King, in sentiment at any rate, is constantly explaining and excusing Malcolm, just as he does the Black Muslims, who terrify him so.[1] He has described elsewhere the visit he paid them, and how they both horrified and fascinated him; he has a presentiment that they are the logical, and maybe inevitable, conclusion of the black revolt, if the whites do not give way—and nothing leads us to believe that they will. In that case, threatens Baldwin, the fire, next time!

[1] I am well aware that Malcolm broke with the Black Muslims, and that it is perhaps they who are responsible for his assassination; there is still no fundamental doctrinal difference between them.

THE BLACK MAN

Malcolm's message is no different: the fire. Only, he adds that it is useless to wait, that the time has come, and from now on the rest is just talk, an attempt to "put off the evil day," and therefore a betrayal of the black people who can wait no longer.

More than this: the second attitude is not merely consecutive to the first, following on from it in a temporal connection; the two are also linked by the strictest internal logic. The dual movement towards rejection of the oppressor and assertion of himself, that we now observe in the revolutionary, is the exact inverse of the oppressed man's habitual attitude: that of self-rejection and hero-worship of the oppressor.

For King, as for Baldwin still, the black American is an American citizen, like the others; at least by rights: his ideal and his only solution, his duty and his rightful ambition is to resemble his white fellow citizens. The late Richard Wright, author of *Black Boy*, the finest Negro protest of our times, would nevertheless always claim: "I am first of all an American!" In other words, whatever difference there may be between blacks and whites, it should not be emphasized; in any case it is often an illusion. In fact, like all oppressed peoples, the black Americans began by rejecting themselves as blacks in so far as was possible, and even more than it was really in their power to do. We see this in those pathetic scenes described by Richard Wright in his account of the Bandung assembly: the black women who tried desperately to uncurl their hair, and spent a fortune on so-called magic powder to whiten their skin. They were trying to efface their own characteristics, so as to be able to assume those of their white heroines; and they strove to emulate the whites to the point of assimilation in order to become perfect American citizens, that is, necessarily, white Americans.

Of course, all these efforts are in vain. One cannot tear one's very nature up by the roots like this, nor is it possible to live in self-hatred unscathed. The black, in despair, returns again and again to this loss of identity. *Nobody Knows My Name* is the title of one of Baldwin's books. Above all, the white man has never accepted the black's emulation. This is a fact we must never lose sight of: the oppressor is the first to refuse assimilation; later the victims of oppression themselves give up the attempt, and it is then that people like Malcolm X appear. The white man has never permitted this love and admiration of himself: so, in his turn, he must submit to the sarcasm and violence that he so nonchalantly dispensed to others. And this time there is nothing he can do about it; the oppressor may discourage love, but he is powerless against the hatred he has himself aroused; all he can do is add fuel to the flames. Malcolm is the poisoned fruit of the blacks' hatred, a hatred born of a great and unrequited love. Malcolm's violence, finally, however terrifying or however questionable it may be, is the inevitable reply to the refusal with which the blacks' demands have so long been met.

I must admit now that it is not easy for me wholeheartedly to defend Malcolm X. Because of a certain tendency to act the demagogue, that I hate to find even in an oppressed creature, because of his racism, and—why should I not be frank about it?—because of his anti-Semitism. Too bad. Not the least of the misfortunes caused by oppression is that the oppressed come to hate each other: the rivalry between Jews and Arabs is one of the most regrettable illogicalities in the history of oppression; at best, the proletariat of the different European countries showed little sympathy for the struggling colonies; and domestic servants are rarely on the side of the proletariat. Without wanting to excuse such grave mistakes, we have been obliged to consider each category of oppression separately, and to accept its struggle as it is, with all its deviations. We must agree that, in spite of his excesses and demagogical misjudgments, Malcolm is a genuine revolutionary, and the true spokesman of the black American revolt. Its aspirations, of which he has a just intuition, and of which he is the personification, are still confused and uncertain, but will most likely tend to clarify themselves in the direction he indicates.

It is within the same perspective, I believe, that we must understand what we can only call the *mythology* he offers his race, and which many have already adopted with enthusiasm, even though for us it is scandalous or incredible. For Malcolm X the final battle has begun; it is not, as Baldwin thinks, merely imminent; nor is it, as King sees it, a game of skill, endurance and evasion tactics. It is a real conflict, a battle to the death; it is being fought with clubs and with dogs, and from time to time murder is committed, though the blacks for the moment are not in a position to retaliate. In the meantime they have to prepare for the showdown, and above all to raise the morale of their troops. How better than by giving them an exalted idea of themselves and of their mission? I do not approve of relying on myths, any more than I do of demogogy, but where could a better source of self-respect be found than in these folk fables? What war leader has not known this temptation in times of crisis? Is it not above all precisely when his followers get discouraged that they should be offered a new image of themselves—an image all the more glorious, the longer their previous existence in contemptuous cultural anonymity.

So we are to witness the revelation, albeit exaggerated beyond measure, of a new black and a new white, who will be the true black and the true white, at last discovered and made known to the world. The greater his past wretchedness, the more the black's *negritude* must now be made to appear desirable.[1] And the greater the deceit practiced by the white, the stronger the need to reduce him to the lowest of the low. The whole structure of the universe has to be recast to meet this new emergency: the past and the future, art and metaphysics;

[1] There is no doubt that the myth-image of *negritude* is a driving force in this revolution.

the first man was black, and the man of the future will be black, even to God himself, who has always been black, not white, as those ignorant, tendentious commentators of Holy Writ would have him.

These are myths, to be sure! A sort of mass delirium, as disastrous as those of the oppressor! That much is certain, and Baldwin, the artist and thinker, is terrified at the discovery, and speaks of it sadly and sometimes in anger. But if we are dealing with myths, they are more correctly counter-myths, the crazed reaction to the accuser's own folly. The white is a horrible monster, asserts Malcolm, and the black an angel; an African writer had already explained to us that all civilization is of black origin; it had to be, since the whites had turned the blacks into monsters and had imposed themselves as the ideal of culture, beauty and truth. Malcolm only wants to unmask an imposture: justice and logic were diametrically opposed to it. History had taken a wrong turning, and a revolution was necessary.

And, after all, what alternative have we been offered? King's policy of love is scarcely less myth-inspired than Malcolm's open violence. Is there not something quite unrealistic in the attempt to solve the blacks' problem "by disturbing the self-satisfaction of the whites"? To disarm the oppressor by loving him in spite of himself? It is as if, at that depth of distress, the victims of oppression cannot live without fantasies. Hence the importance of religion among all the black leaders: King is a minister, as were his father and grandfather before him; Baldwin has preached in the pulpit; Malcolm abjures Christianity, only to adopt another religion—Islam. This business of the conversion of so many black revolutionaries to Mohammedanism has been a cause of much argument, surprise and ironic comments. Yet it seems to me something quite simple: *Mohammedanism acts as an exact counter-myth to Christianity.* To be sure, it is also the religion of many colonized Africans (as time

THE BLACK MAN

goes on the black Americans will tend more and more to compare themselves with the Africans)[1] whereas Christianity is *par excellence* the religion of the white oppressor. In the hands of the Black Muslims, however, Mohammedanism also becomes something fantastic, and it is by no means certain that Mohammedans in other parts of the world could still recognize their own religion in this universe of black angels and white devils.

Probably in order to counter the extraordinary racial segregation, which has split the most highly industrialized country in the world from top to bottom, at least a miracle was needed. To dare attack so apparently impregnable a position, they needed the battering ram of the most powerfully destructive myths; at the very least, radical condemnation of the white and a new Messianic religion which favored the blacks. The Hebrews needed the Column of Fire and the offer of the Promised Land to persuade them to leave Egypt, and these myths have been revived in their entirety by present-day Zionists. Without them, where can the oppressed, who has lived so long in subjection, ever find the strength to break with his slavery? At the thought of the revolt he must undertake, in the face of so powerful an enemy, how otherwise will he not feel spiritually as naked and vulnerable as he is physically, with no weapons in his hands? Only the assurance that he has a magic ship, and will win his place in the great Black Man's Heaven, the only true Paradise, will help him face the storm he has himself been forced to loose, but which threatens to overwhelm both him and his oppressor.

In actual fact, King and Malcolm draw on two myths, or two counter-myths born out of the affliction of the black American. Both of them demand freedom and dignity for their people, but they each translate in their own way one or another of the an-

---

[1] The Afro-American movement founded by Malcolm just before his death is perhaps just another myth; or, a stroke of genius; at any rate, it offers one way out of an impossible situation.

swers that the down-trodden black can give his oppressor. King hopes to disarm the whites by a great act of love, repeated over and over until the two races fuse and become one. There is nothing absurd in this so long as there remains a hope that the white man will finally consent to this love. In the meantime, King's patience and his dreams certainly help to pass the time of waiting. But how can one ever expect the oppressor's consent, when in the contract that seals their union he must sign away his privileges? Even without taking into account the horror for white Americans of having to abandon the image they have created of themselves and of America. Historically speaking, nights like the fourth of August in France are rare, or else mere illusions. It is not often that they can prevent the victim from discovering that his patience is in vain, or hinder the revolt from taking its course. Malcolm is purely the embodiment of this intuition, on the verge of despair, that all is useless; *revolt is first of all the acknowledgment of an impossible situation.*

Then, of course, comes the period of extremism. And certainly the revolt destroys—perhaps forever—all hope of integration: the revolutionary quite clearly stands for permanent segregation. Was he not already cut off? Whose fault is it if the only hope of salvation he can see now lies in divorce and violence? Later perhaps there will be a return to Baldwin's way of thinking, to a greater lucidity in self-examination and in the understanding of one's own people and of others. Meanwhile, once he has entered the fray, the revolutionary can hardly be expected to judge himself justly, when he has been so unjustly crushed and humiliated, so that his retaliation must transcend all justice.

(Translated by Jane Brooks)

(Introduction to the French edition of James Baldwin's
The Fire Next Time, Gallimard, 1963.)

2

A Total Revolt

We have by now learned that oppressed people resemble each other. Their own peculiar features and individual history aside, colonized peoples, Jews, women, the poor show a kind of family likeness; all bear a burden which leaves the same bruises on their soul, and similarly distorts their behavior. A like suffering often produces similar gestures, similar expressions of pain, the same inner paroxysms, the same agony or the same revolt.

We all feel slight hesitation in placing the black American in this portrait gallery, and the fault is not entirely ours. Black Americans are certainly an oppressed race; we could guess as much from their music, and it is apparent in the comedies of the American Belle Epoque, where blacks were always portrayed as servants, elevator operators and shoe-shine boys, never as heroes and never in positions of authority. And yet, though it is difficult to explain, they made songs of their distress and it was for us something loveable. Their slightly servile humility, their childish terrors, which made the great whites of their eyes roll and their knees knock together like castanets, and their pidgin-English, all this made us laugh. There was nothing pitiful or threatening about them. At any rate this was the picture that American screen-writers wanted to put over to us. Later we really came to know them, as G.I.'s, as well-built, well-fed and well-dressed as their white counterparts. Laughing, they offered us canned meat, and we were grateful for it. They did, so the rumor went, have a few minor problems: in the mess, for instance, a drunken white soldier would call them niggers, and this strangely sent them into towering rages; pig-headedly, they persisted in courting the blondest women, who obviously repulsed their advances. But at the same time the patriotic films of the period taught us that the black man, though insulted, behaved nobly like a loyal comrade: under enemy fire he would save the life of the white man, now sober and wounded, and receive his apologies. By his constant devotion, he would at last touch the heart of the blond woman, who would consent to go for a drive with him in his luxury automobile (the same model as the white man's). In short, in this Land of Cockaigne even the least fortunate were not really to be pitied. The great American democracy would, with the passing of time, take it upon itself to raise them to the others' level.

It is true, I had almost forgotten the lynchings; from time to time we would be made uncomfortable by news of a bewildering occurrence: a black man would be captured by an hysterical crowd, lynched, hung, sprayed with gasoline and burned. It was so extraordinary that we could not quite believe our ears. The two pictures: the one of a prosperous, free and democratic America, the other of these mediaeval bonfires, could not be reconciled, and so, as quickly as we could, we forgot about the second one. And anyway, all that happened in the South, a fossil land dreaming of past glories; a people not lacking in charm, with their colonial mansions and their benevolent paternalism, but who, embittered and frustrated by their defeat, must suddenly have gone crazy. Here again, we knew of a solution; it was actually a black writer who had suggested it to us. We had all read the story of Richard Wright's *Black Boy,* who went north to escape the reactionary madness of the South. The real America, the land of equality, efficiency, modernity, was in the North. In order to live a man's life and not a nigger's, all you had to do was go there. If salvation was at hand, even a few days away by train, then there was no cause for despair.

Well, we were wrong; once again, thoughtlessly, we had drawn conclusions about someone's misfortunes before hearing him plead his own case. The pictures that were drawn for us were false because they were incomplete and did not correspond with each other; and above all, because we did not know what they really meant for the American Negro. Thanks to James Baldwin and to his wonderfully concise, yet poetic, writing, expressed in a language so extraordinarily rich and condensed that several readings of his book are necessary to grasp all its allusions, henceforth we know that *the black American is one of the chief victims of oppression.*

> "Elijah, I should imagine, has had nothing to lose since the day he saw his father's blood rush out—rush down, and splash, so the legend has it, down through the leaves of a tree, on him. But neither did the other men around the table have anything to lose."

There he has given us the key-word of all great oppressions: it is a fearful revelation for the oppressed when he understands that he has nothing to lose, and it is a critical time in the life of a nation when a section of its population decides that it has nothing to lose. All the obligations of society and all the patterns of community life can suddenly no longer be taken for granted. After all, we had thought that those vexations or embarrassing incidents that from time to time marred the relations of black and white Americans did not profoundly affect their essential unity as a nation. Good-will on both sides and some readjustments could put everything right. The blacks might

moderate their impatience, for instance, and not try to force
their way too hastily into the schools; the whites could make an
effort to be generous and open the doors a crack for them . . .
Complete and final refusal is only expressed by a few individuals, declared Robert Kennedy, when he was Attorney-Gen-
eral. No, replies Baldwin, it is not a matter of a few individuals;
some readjustments will not do. It is the whole of American
society that excludes, martyrizes and kills the black man. The
good-will paraded by the North only pointlessly confuses the
issue. Hence the slogan: everything, and now—which would
seem exaggerated and foolish if one did not admit that *the
black American is oppressed by the whole of American society*.

Of course, it will be said that Baldwin is overstating things.
Seriously, how can the black American, citizen of a rich and a
free country, have so much to complain about? But people are
always accused of exaggeration when they describe injustices
to those who do not want to hear about them. We were told
often enough that we were exaggerating when we tried to tell
the French what their colonies were suffering, and to warn
them of what was inevitable and imminent. While we are on
the subject, let us refute this nonsense once and for all: of
course, serious oppression is possible even within a context of
relative prosperity. Are not women oppressed sometimes even
in the midst of opulence? Black Americans are, paradoxically,
down-trodden rich Americans; many African blacks who have
now achieved independence would be glad to have their standard of living; but the fact still remains that the black American
takes a dramatic view of his situation. At all events we must
beware of making the mistake common to the bourgeois and
Marxists alike of laying too much stress on the material aspect.
Oppression is like an octopus: it is hard to tell which of its
arms has the tightest strangle-hold. Injustice, insults, humiliation and insecurity can be as hard to bear as hunger. Even if
their misfortune is not as great as they make out—an opinion
I do not subscribe to—it is already bad enough that black

THE BLACK MAN

Americans should feel and think of themselves as Baldwin describes: "Negroes in this country . . . are taught really to despise themselves from the moment their eyes open on the world."

Everything seems calculated to convince them of this: the world is white and they are black; power, wealth, pleasure, ideas, art are white; even God is white. How then can the black man not think himself an inferior being? He is afraid of this too powerful universe, not made for him; unarmed to combat its ill-will. Moreover, this anguish he feels in confronting the white man's world is nurtured in him from birth by his own people; they fear the white man will take vengeance on him, even annihilate him physically, if he does not quickly learn to submit. The black man's fear, his shaking knees and great rolling eyes, correspond then to a certain reality, but should no longer make us laugh. Worse than physical damage, worse than beatings, than professional exclusion, worse even than death in his spiritual ruin, wherein he consents to his own abasement. For he ends by accepting what the whites tell him and believing in it; and from then on he is lost. He actually becomes the stupid lackey, the comic shoe-shine boy; a domestic animal, or, as Baldwin says, a kind of saint. We have already met the well-behaved colonized, the Good Spirit. He becomes in reality, like them, an accessory after the fact of his own oppression.

No doubt the new generation, Baldwin's own and particularly that of his juniors, no longer wants to believe that it is forever inferior, and will no longer be content to take the back seat assigned to it. But where will this lead them? If they deny the accusations, these become all the more intolerable. The former generation had many saints, or cowards, among its numbers—the present one is overflowing with aggrieved and humiliated men, filled with a perpetual rage and torment, who despise their race and detest themselves. Baldwin's contempt and hatred of his own father, even tempered by pity, is truly unbearable. And as life is unlivable with such poison in the heart, they seek oblivion in alcohol, in drugs and in crime. This is merely another form of destruction. Saintliness or permanent humiliation, such is their dilemma. It is not so easy to escape oppression.

I have been trying to play the Devil's Advocate. In fact, the situation of the black American is not only a matter of opinions and prejudices that are offensive to him, and humiliating by what they reveal of the white man's character. It arises too from events and institutions that are very real and very hard to bear, that weigh on him from day to day, distort his relations with his fellow-citizens and give an air of fatality to the outcome of his struggle, a game already lost and won.

> "You must consider what happens to this citizen . . . search, in his shoes, for a job, for a place to live; ride, in his skin, on segregated buses; see, with his eyes, the signs saying 'White' and 'Colored,' and especially the signs that say 'White Ladies' and 'Colored *Women';* look into the eyes of his wife; look into the eyes of his son . . ."

You need a lot of imagination to put yourself in someone else's place; and it is astonishing how much we can find bearable for others. We have known about all that for a long time, but we have never lost a night's sleep over it; nor is it the most important part of what Baldwin teaches us. So we shall pass over these many subtle, "minor" unpleasantnesses, and how the Negro puts up with, or does not put up with them; as well as the more or less explicit prohibitions against drinking in certain cafés, bathing in certain pools, staying in certain hotels and going to certain movie-houses, etc. For those who do not like this kind of mental exercise, more objective facts must be given, I suppose; they are easier to grasp. A few years ago an American sociologist embarked on a systematic study of American jurisdiction, state by state. He was forced with horror to conclude that *racism is legal in the United States.* A circular, dated July, 1942, gives orders to "see to it that men of different

THE BLACK MAN

races are not without necessity put together in dormitories or at the same table in refectories." It is signed: Eisenhower. In 1948, the same man declared that "a certain degree of segregation was necessary in the army." Mixed marriages were clearly considered criminal in many states, and were punished as such. Usually about one fifth of young Americans fail to find work; the proportion of young blacks is about one third. Black Americans form a ninth of the total population; the population of their professional elite is infinitely far removed from this relative figure. With reference to this last point, we all know the following objection, widely raised today: "That clearly proves that the oppressed, or formerly oppressed, class is not up to it! There is no reason to offer them jobs they don't deserve and would do badly, nor to appoint black teachers and doctors just because they are black; now it is you who are being paternalistic." Hard-pressed colonial advocates had already hit on this notion and used it as their last argument, and there is certainly many a good soul whom it leaves perplexed. There is no shadow of a doubt, now, that there are not enough high-ranking technicians and cadres in the Congo and elsewhere. But the scarcity of a professional elite among blacks, and their frequently poor training, after decades of colonization, is surely one of the most scandalous proofs of oppression and race prejudice. Unless we add that they are by nature incapable of making decent technicians and conscientious doctors . . . in which case we are back with racism once again. Further, if the professional elite among black Americans is smaller than in other categories of the population, they still have a relatively far greater number of unemployed overall; are they then not even worthy of manual labor?

To sum up, if we define total oppression as a state which affects the human being in all aspects of his existence, in the way he sees himself and in the way others see him, in his various entrees into urban society, and in his future in history, then the oppression of the American Negro is undeniably a total op-

pression. A product of the whole of American society, it affects
the whole of the black man's existence. If we look closer, we
see that there is no one aspect of his life, no single action of his,
that is not thrown off balance by this fundamental aggression.
The battles at the entrances of southern universities showed a
shocked world that you have to be a hero to pursue higher education when you have the insolence to be an ambitious black
man. He cannot even be poor like others (for the big automobile myth does not rule out slums, beetles and bugs). In a way
he is doubly poor; he is the poor man among the poor whites,
who are crueler than the rich because they need to maintain
and to widen the pathetic distance which separates them.

As with most oppressions of one people by another, we discover here an inexorable process of systematic elimination. The
fundamental desire of the white man, whether disguised or
openly confessed, is to remove the black from his sight entirely. And, as Baldwin in this manifesto of his is staking his last
chance, he follows his idea through to its conclusion: *in the
final analysis what the white hopes for is the annihilation of the
black.* There is no reason why the Americans should not one
day attempt against their blacks what the Germans, another
white, Christian nation, attempted against the Jews. Once
again the reader is bound to protest when he reads this pitiless
indictment. I believe, on the contrary, that Baldwin had
glimpsed here a terrifying truth: just as pogroms were no acci-
dent in Jewish history, but the sign of an endemic disease,
exacerbated and coming to a head, so lynchings, hangings and
bonfires are the final explosion of the true sentiments of the
white man with regard to the black man.

Henceforth, we can scarcely be surprised by the conclusion
to which we are ineluctably brought; nor by the new answer
that the younger generation of black men are now preparing.
Their elders have tried all the false escape routes and none has
saved them: not submission, nor hatred, nor economic repres-
sion, not religion nor the Church, adds Baldwin, who has

preached from the pulpit. No solution is workable while the context remains the same. Since the whole of American society questions the existence of the black man, the existence of this society must in turn be called in question. To combat a total oppression, he calls for *a total revolt*.

Total revolt is the result of a situation where those who revolt, having no longer anything to protect, are no longer restrained in any way. Neither by the fear of death, nor, which is perhaps more serious still, by the respect of values they share with the oppressor. Total revolt means war, the discovery of violence and of the terror it inspires. We saw on television the other evening one of the leaders of the Black Muslims; this man filled us with horror by his overwhelming hatred of white men, by his cold-blooded determination to eliminate them all one day if he has the power. It is impossible to deny the accuracy of his anlaysis: that the mere fear which the blacks might eventually arouse would have the power to drive back the oppressor. A high price must surely be paid for such a revolt, but: "A people from whom everything has been taken away, including, most crucially, their sense of their own worth [will do] anything to regain it . . . for, at the very worst, I would merely have contributed to the destruction of a house I hated, and it would not matter if I perished, too. One has been perishing here so long."

Total revolt means also immoral, or rather amoral, warfare, fought under the one standard left: that of liberty. It is an unprincipled war, for principles have too long been used to mystify and grind down the oppressed. Let the reader look carefully at Baldwin's pages on the Catholic Church. Since in slavery nothing was possible, in revolt everything is allowed. Even the worst, the most evil deeds. For what is the meaning of "evil"? The underdog was never asked his opinion of these fake definitions. The search for new standards and for a new order can begin after the cataclysm. This is why colonized races in revolt had no program; and why, with others, the

Black Muslims offer such a Utopian future. Doubtless, if they had a foothold on the heights of power, they would think in more realistic terms. For the moment, they are the mystical, but fully satisfying, expression of the rift in American society. Their bitter, extremist demands are no more than the exigency of desperation in the face of a desperate situation.

Baldwin, as a writer and as a man, refuses for his part to follow them this far. He has white friends, to some of whom he would entrust his life; he advocates mixed marriages, and would fight if necessary against the fanaticism of the Black Muslims. Yet there is one point we should not lose sight of: the wild schemes of the Black Muslim demagogues apart, there is no fundamental difference between them and the most moderate of black Americans. The truth is that all blacks suffer the same oppression, and that now they have all come to believe that it must end: they all demand a structural transformation of the nation and a modification of its values. The Black Muslims suddenly discovered that God was black and that the white man was a demon who must be wiped out to leave room for the black man, the only true creature of God. Is Baldwin saying anything different, when he suggests, calmly and with apparent mental balance, that America should cease to consider itself as a white nation?

I must admit that after reading his book, I am more scared than Baldwin himself. He wants to believe that the threat is still postponed: The fire next time. Blacks and whites of goodwill can still unite to ward off the catastrophe. The question is, how. If we reverse his negative proposition, we obtain the following: the Americans must consent to becoming a nation of half-breeds. But either we are very much mistaken, or else the white Americans, those of the North included, are as far as they can possibly be from such an upheaval. Not that the idea is a product of delirium, for if we exclude partition (which is what the Black Muslims are calling for) there seems no other way out. After all, that would have been the real solution to the colonial tragedies of our era: an accelerated interpenetration of the races. But no colonizer, however broad-minded, however progressive, even dreamed of it. Perhaps there are moments in the history of nations when they cannot but be blind and deaf, though war and destruction are at their door. If Baldwin's description is true—and he is too convincing for it to be otherwise —catastrophe is now brewing in the very heart of the American nation.

An irreversible change has apparently taken place in America: the black American now knows who he is and what his true place is among his fellow citizens. *When the oppressed has seen the extent of his oppression in this way, then it becomes unbearable to him.* Once the victim of oppression has had a glimpse of the possibility of freedom, and agrees to pay the price for it, it is useless to hope for an enduring peace. If Baldwin has stated the problem correctly: either a nation of halfbreeds, or war, then I am really very afraid for America and the Americans.

(Translated by Jane Brooks)

(Written for a sociological study published by
Editions Anthropos, 1968.) To Léopold Sédar Senghor.

3

Negritude and Jewishness

In attempting to confront the several facets of his Jewish identity, Albert Memmi discovered that there is only one word in French to describe this state—judaisme (Judaism). There are no equivalents for the English words Jewishness or Jewry. In coining words to make good these omissions, Memmi realized that the value lay not in the words themselves but in the concepts they embraced. This led him to a further study of the black peoples and their own efforts to realize their changing status in the contemporary world. (TRANSLATOR'S NOTE)

I

I wish to define more fully the words Jewishness, Jewry and Judaism. Allow me to recall very briefly that, having decided in a previous book to render an account of myself as a Jew, I quickly felt the need of a word which, to the exclusion of all others, expressed the fact of being Jewish. I realized with astonishment and perplexity that this word did not exist in French, or more precisely, I found that *judaisme* had too many other connotations to be used with precision and without ambiguity. I decided therefore to create a specific term—I chose *judéité* (Jewishness).[1]

I should like to stress that this discovery did not come from a conscious attempt to analyze the Jewish state; it sprang, on the contrary, from a methodological need to grapple with a complex reality which was still escaping me. It was only in clarifying the reality of the Jewish existence, in examining separately each dimension, that I was led: to find as exclusive and adequate a definition for Jewishness as possible; thereby to distinguish it from other dimensions; finally, to distinguish between these different dimensions and to define each one separately.

It is inevitable, with a subject that has always aroused the most intense passions and caused the most varied reflections, that definitions can be interpreted in different ways, but this should not contradict the very principle of these distinctions. On the contrary, we have even more need of order in a matter which is so greatly confused. Today, I am still not sure whether, with these three definitions, I have exhausted the three dimensions of the Jewish reality, and I will readily allow them to be contested. However, I am even more convinced that they had to be distinguished by trying as many different approaches as possible.

There was no need to reflect very long to ascertain that the term Judaism was, at the same time, too rich and too vague in its meaning. It was too restricting and inefficient for exacting an objective usage. It meant, sometimes, all the traditional, religious and moral values which ruled the collective life of the Jews; and, sometimes, the Jewish community; it meant the belonging of a Jewish individual to his group; and the measure

[1] I should like here to express my deepest thanks to Professor Maurice de Gandillac who strengthened my determination to take this linguistic and conceptual departure.

of his traditional beliefs; and even, since the foundation of Zionism, his adherence to Jewish values which were not necessarily religious. Obviously, it was better to assign only one of these meanings to this word, and to find new terms for the others. A little order, even at the risk of an apparent impoverishment of the word itself, could only be beneficial. It seemed to me that the most reasonable meaning for Judaism must be that of the sum of the cultural and religious traditions.

I realized as soon as I tried to categorize the Jewish condition more completely, that it was necessary to pursue this definition further. One has to be able to distinguish, within this cultural whole, between the solely religious heritage and the ethical regulations which constitute the moral philosophy of the Jews.[1] In any case, the most urgent and most immediately apparent need, for easier reference and study, was to be able to consider separately the Jewish ideology and its works on the one side; and the Jewish people and the groups who conformed more or less to this ideology, and who lived more or less within its dictates, on the other.

The word *judacité* (Jewry) should mean a group of Jews. But taking into account the geographical distribution of the Jews, we must be able to give it both a wide and a narrow meaning. Jewry thus means the whole of the Jewish community, and, remembering how this Jewry is spread out in many communities throughout the world, it also means each of the

---

[1] By the word Judaism must one also mean the inventions of contemporary Jewish thinkers and essayists, who, by setting out in a certain way to prolong this cultural tradition, give to it an almost new look? It is a serious problem, at least for the specialist, to know what precisely constitutes Jewish heritage. Whether it does possess a definite and in some way confining unity, or whether it would embrace evolving ideas, which would enrich it but transform it in the course of time. All the same, so as not to make more work, I thought it wise for the time being, to include with this same term, the institutions which organize the collective life of the Jews, and which, in part, spring from its values, but which, to my mind, inspire them in return.

local Jewries; for example, French Jewry, or American Jewry. But the most important thing to remember is the demographical meaning: Jewry stands for a group of Jewish people.

Finally, *judéité* (Jewishness) would mean simply the way for a Jew to be both subjectively and objectively Jewish. The way in which he feels himself to be a Jew, and in which he confronts the Jewish condition.

Of course, in a sociological perspective, I cannot claim an existence which is actually separate from Jewishness. Indeed, it seems to me absurd to contemplate the Jewish values separately, since they obviously would not exist without the Jewish group, and, more precisely, without the socio-historic events which have molded its particular destiny. In this respect, I maintain that Judaism is the ideology and the institutional whole of Jewry. And, that almost always Jewishness contains a more or less definite *reference* to the traditional Jewish values, whether this reference is conscious or unconscious. In relation to Jewry, Jewishness is the degree of conformity, both objective and subjective. And to conclude the triangle, it is clear that belonging to a group is rarely confined to simple mechanical solidarity, purely negative in the face of danger; belonging to a group always means to some extent the recognition of that group's values.[1]

It follows, and this is what I want to stress, that Jewishness can vary in its intensity and even in its elements from one individual to another, according to the particular make-up of each subject. This is why I have been able to talk about the *coefficient of Jewishness*[2] with my colleagues. Bearing in mind

[1] I said that it was not my intention here to expand the concept of Jewishness; it would have been necessary to give equal consideration to the reference to the Gentiles, which is very important, since this is at the root of the negative side of Jewishness. This dimension particularly struck Sartre in his "Reflections on the Jewish Question." Probably because he is surrounded by Jewish friends and colleagues, who feel that they no longer have hardly any positive attachment.

[2] See in particular "Récherches sur la judéité," in *Revue Française de Sociologie*, Paris, janvier-mars 1965.

the precaution that one must take in using a mathematical expression to define such a rich and fluent reality, we even tried to establish the criteria for reckoning this coefficient. Whatever this is, one must be able to consider the Jewishness of each subject separately.

In summing up, I should like to distinguish clearly between the definitions which may have seemed somewhat confused. First, there is the Jewish *group,* or *Jewry.* Next, its *values,* or *Judaism.* Finally, the *degree of conformity* of the Jew to his group on the one hand and to its values on the other, or *Jewishness.*

I have given a detailed assessment of these three terms. Here, as a reminder, are the definitions.

Jewry is *a group of Jewish persons;* be it in the widest sense, all the Jews throughout the world, or in the narrowest sense, a group of Jews identified by location, for example French Jewry or New York Jewry.

Judaism is *the whole of the teachings, beliefs and institutions of the Jews* whether they are established or not, written or spoken; in sum, the values of the organization which constitutes and rules the life of a Jewish group; or again, Jewish culture in the widest sense: collective customs, religion, philosophy, jurisdiction and arts.

Jewishness is *the fact and manner of being a Jew;* all the objective, sociological, psychological and biological characteristics which make a Jew; the way in which a Jew lives, and at the same time his belonging to Jewry and his integration with the non-Jewish world.

II

Let us now come to the parallel with Negritude. It is interesting to note that the situation presented itself to me in the same manner as it would have done to a black man. It sprang from

the need to describe, to outline and to define my personality as
a Jew; that is to say, among other things, in relation to the collective personality of the group to which I belonged. Now the
Jewish group has lived in special and oppressive circumstances
which made it difficult for them to look at themselves objectively—illusions were born of the accusations of others and
through self-rejection, just as myths were created to counter
the accusations. Obviously this abnormal condition of oppression cannot be compared to that of people who are masters of
their own destiny, for whom the relationship between religion
and culture, for example, has taken a totally different form.[1]
The notion of Negritude came from the same need. It recognized the separation of the black, and summed it up conven-
iently in one word, presenting itself, as it were, as a flag for
liberation and a reconquest of the self.

But it would have been surprising if such a word which expressed and illustrated the condition of the black man, its benefits, and its deficiencies, its revolts and its hopes at the same
time, had not revealed all the trouble and the difficulties.

Aimé Césaire, who is, to my knowledge, the founder of this
word in French, defined it in beautiful but essentially poetic
language.[2] It was left to L. S. Senghor to attempt to formulate
the definitions. When Senghor defines Negritude as, "All the
cultural values of the black world, as they are expressed [3] in the
lives, the institutions and the world of the black people," his
definition corresponds to what I have proposed to call Judaism. It means the cultural and religious traditions as they are
realized by living men today, not by individuals and by groups

[1] See *The Colonizer and the Colonized,* Orion Press, New York.

[2] I have been told that there is a more precise definition of Negritude
by Aimé Césaire in the magazine *Tropiques,* where the first essays on
Negritude appeared. Unfortunately, I have not been able to obtain a
copy. In any case, Aimé Césaire and L. S. Senghor do not contradict
each other on this subject.

[3] This definition was printed most recently in "Liberté 1—Négritude
et humanisme . . ." Editions du Seuil, Paris 1966. The exchanges at the
Dakar Festival did not change it at all.

Negritude and Jewishness

as such. Now when he adds, "Our only difficulty has been to confront this Negritude and to broaden its meaning by our own example," he means then the equivalent of Jewishness, that is to say the *way of living* with and dealing with these values.

When the organizers of the Dakar Meeting (an annual meeting of black intellectuals) announce it as "The General States of Negritude" (Alioune Diop), this time they apparently mean by Negritude an assembly of men, and even an exhaustive assembly, judging, at least, by its representation. The proof of this is that the discussion turned on this point. This time Negritude was used as the word Jewry.

When another organizer declared that "Negritude has to be defended and glorified" we do not know whether he is referring to the men or to their values; probably to the values this time, since the official title "Festival of Negro Arts" corresponds better to the values. Although this title is very restricting if one acknowledges that a culture is not summed up in its arts. More especially since we talk of "Negro humanism" and of its contribution to "universal civilization" (Senghor). Let us admit that there was here a vacillation between men and culture.

Of course, we must not carry this systematic naïveté too far; in fact, in a confused way, Negritude has come to mean at one and the same time a group of black men, the values of the black world, and the adherence of each man and of each group to this world and to these values. As I often said in reference to the tripartite concept of Judaism, in reality we are not dealing with three tightly shut drawers, each one containing clearly defined contents. But is it not therefore even more necessary to have at our disposal sufficient tools to handle each aspect of the black man's existence?

We see it clearly in the unrest and anger of the younger generation; with all this talk about Negritude and black humanity, they say with indignation, men are beginning to be forgotten in favor of their values. All black men are far from being nation-

THE BLACK MAN

ally liberated, and in the new black nations, not all black men are socially free. After the colonizer, or at the same time as he, or even with his help: "Today, Negroes exploit Negroes!" Today, "we are living in the age of Tshombe!"

There is no doubt that the setting up of nations in large sections of the black world is helping to dispense with the negative aspects of the black man's life, just as the foundation of the State of Israel has so successfully stamped out Jewish negativism, so much so that some all too forgetful Jews doubt that it ever existed. And we understand that the natives of Senegal and the Ivory Coast, from now on masters of their fate, at least their political fate, wish to stress only the positive aspects of black values and black art. From now on they only wish to remember the affirmative and even glorious side. But if it is true that the oppression of the black world has lessened, it has still not disappeared. And such euphoria can seem premature and a little detached, if not insulting to those for whom Negritude is still more of a burden than a source of happiness. This is the origin of the uneasy dissatisfaction that many participants at the Dakar Meeting felt; here were the beginnings of a new kind of conflict, within the black race, between those who were secure and those who were not. And we understand that the organizers preferred not to invite certain nations: the South Africans for example, and even the Guineans and the Cubans; these are the people who would probably insist on recalling that there are still negative aspects to the black condition.

From this there springs the revolt of the young people against this total euphoria and against the whole world. If the affirmation of the positive aspects of the values of the black man must obscure his miseries, then they must denounce these false values: "A backward-looking culture." "A paralyzed history!" "The tom-toms of Césaire's and Senghor's Negritude murmur like cracked cauldrons!"

The High Commissioner of Dahomey said just that: "Negritude will be the liberator, or it will not exist." In his harsh re-

volt against the fate of the blacks, the black American writer
LeRoi Jones has come to question the existence of any black
culture: "Black culture does not exist."

It is difficult for a white man to interfere in one of the most
grave internal conflicts to upset the black world. And if I allow
myself to take part in such a discussion, it is not only because I
believe in the virtue of a certain rationality, even in the most
passionate of debates; it is simply, I repeat, because it seems to
be of interest to compare the fate of the blacks with the Jewish
fate at this point. And in the hope that a methodological proposal, which has greatly helped me in one case, can give similar
help to another; it will be necessary then to split the concept of
Negritude, as I was obliged to split that of Judaism.

Negritude is still largely negative and must be recognized as
such; if not it becomes deceptive. The end of self-rejection is
certainly still premature for the black man today, but con-
versely it would be catastrophic not to acknowledge the values
of the blacks whether they exist now, or in the past, or are at
the point of establishing themselves, just because the condition
of the black man remains so wretched.[1] One sees all the danger
when one reads in the declaration of the same High Commissioner of Dahomey that "Africa needs the workman's hammer
before the sculptor's chisel . . . Africa will sing her most beautiful song only when she is free!" On this point he is probably
not absolutely mistaken. However, he is speaking of two differ-

[1] Besides, the blacks are absolutely appalled when they hear this
theory from the whites, even when they are good friends. This happened to Sartre. In one of his best essays: "Black Orpheus," this author,
without altogether omitting a reference to black culture, stressed the
blacks' liking for negativism in Negritude. He insulted many blacks who
admired him and were grateful to him for having helped them to define
themselves. But Sartre had wanted to denounce the oppression of the
blacks, he was therefore led to emphasize the relations between Negritude and the whites. It is thus, I think, that one should read his "Reflections on the Jewish Question." He is speaking as a white man and
as a Gentile, and did not have to concern himself very much with the
positive aspects of Jewishness and Negritude.

ent levels, strongly linked naturally, but it is very important to keep from confusing them. From now on we should be able to distinguish between the past, present and future cultural values, the different black communities with their different sociopolitical problems; and, finally, the manner in which each individual black man approaches these values, conforms to them and rejects them, the way in which he fits into the community, whether he conforms to it or revolts against it. It is imperative to name, and to define separately these states. They are, I propose: Negrity (*négrité*); Negroism (*négrisme*); Negritude (*négritude*).

Negrity would be clearly all black persons and black groups.

Negroism would be the traditional and cultural values of the black peoples.

Negritude, then, would be reserved for the manner of feeling oneself to be a black man, by belonging to a particular group of men and by adherence to its values.

III

Obviously, I do not intend in these few pages to minister to the precise and complex methodological needs which are raised as much by epistemology as by the sociological circumstances. It would be sufficient for me to have been able to point one direction for the research to follow, and to have added a further argument to the hypothesis that there is a similarity in the conditions of most of the oppressed peoples. And may I point out in passing, that one finds the same need, born of the same confusion, in the case of the Muslims. This because the term Muslim means not only all the believers in the religion proposed by Mohammed, but also the religion itself, and the ethical values which ordinarily go along with it. And it is perhaps time to apply certain distinctions here too.

Of course, these parallels do not do away with the specific

meanings of each word, and of its contents, for the main reason that, beyond the similarities, the differences between the conditions and the traditions are of the utmost importance. The oppression of the Jew is not the same as that of the black man, nor as that of the colonized nations. Neither, by the way, is that of each black man with that of all black men. And, furnished with these ideas and with these common tools, it is up to the blacks to make their own inventory. We can only propose the questions: How does one characterize the contents of Negritude, or more exactly, from now on, of each Negritude? If it is agreed, as I proposed, that Negritude is only the degree of conformity of each black man to the collective personality of the group, one can see that this would be an essentially dynamic concept with several variables. What part will the negative and positive aspects play each time? Will we be able to describe and to define a coefficient of Negritude in the way that we found the coefficient of Jewishness?

We shall see, that if the negative-positive argument is at the very core of each individual Negritude, it becomes less important in relation to Negroism, that is to say to the black cultural values.

Strictly speaking, a culture could not be negative; it can be inefficient, broken down, ill-adjusted to the new needs, even contradictory, and spread out according to the geography and the different influences that are brought to bear on it, it could be affected by the least change. This is why I did not speak of the negative side of Judaism, or now of Negroism or of Islam; that would seem absurd, but I propose to distinguish between tradition and culture. To find the means of placing oneself in a true, more or less integrated perspective with the past, or in a functional attitude to its values; to conform to the established religious, ethical or aesthetic norms, or to ignore them, or at least to wish to pass beyond them in favor of a permanent re-creation of rules and of works more consciously adapted to the needs of modern man. Such a variety of reference allows one to go beyond these false problems of all or nothing, of total acceptance or absolute rejection.

However fascinating these problems are, the most important to my mind is this movement of *distinction,* which alone will allow the false and restricting unity to be disposed of in recognition of the several facets of black reality. (In the cultural and social history of the Christians there has been no problem; they quickly drew a line between Christianity and being a Christian. And this has been of great benefit to them.)

The black man must maintain the right to contest his tradition; and he must have the right to keep his distance from his own group. For that, he must be able to distinguish between this tradition and the way he adapts to it, that is to say accepts or rejects it, or more exactly accepts or rejects it in varying degrees. He must be able to accept it sufficiently, without being suffocated by the tradition of his group, or impeded by its revolt; and he must be able to reject it without being forced to reject himself completely. And for all this he must have the right tools.

The words themselves are of little importance, but the concepts seem indispensable to me, however they are expressed. But I do not overlook the fact that these concepts have only temporary use. For example, when all black men have their own independent nations, the word "Negrity" will disappear perhaps or become one with humanity. Because, fundamentally and despite its appearance, Negrity does not correspond to a racial community, but to a community of *condition,*[1] which is a condition of oppression, under the mythical pretext of race. Negrity is simply the ethnic response of the black man to the ethnic accusation of the white. We find the same global and probably provisional response in most of the colonized, who have grown into reactionary racists with pseudo-ethnic solidarity to counter the ethnic contempt of the colonizer.

[1] Another parallel with the Jewish condition.

Negritude and Jewishness

Perhaps finally even the concept of Negroism will be considered useless. Can we speak of a cultural community of blacks throughout the world? Today when blacks are divided between Muslims, Christians, Catholics, Protestants, primitive religions, and even a few Jews, what is this "black humanity" that Senghor refers to, if not principally and always a reference to the color of the skin. For some years, in order to define further this overly precise and restricting ethnic reference, most of the black leaders have insisted on referring to the original *geographic community* of all blacks: Africa. We do not know whether Africa will remain a historical and poetic myth, or whether it will become a political project. It appears that on the eve of his death, Malcolm X dreamed of a veritable convergence of the world's blacks on Africa's doorstep. For Aimé Césaire, the West Indian poet, Mother Africa provided an extraordinarily fertile well of hope. But I do repeat, it is up to the blacks to determine the exact contents of the debate and their relationship with a real or a mythical Africa. We know that the moment they speak of this cultural community, whether it is real or imaginary, they must have a concept at their disposal, or at least an unequivocal word to describe it.

And if one day a reassessment of this terminology becomes necessary again, I shall not be surprised, nor shall I regret it, for I believe in the dynamism of all human groups, and of all conditions. And therefore in the inescapable dynamism of all these concepts, and even perhaps in their periodical death and in their necessary replacement.

(Translated by Ghislaine Boulanger)

II

THE
COLONIZED

(The preface to the 1965 edition of *The Colonizer and the Colonized*.)

4

On the Colonizer and the Colonized

It would be untrue to say that I foresaw the full significance of this book in 1957 when I wrote it. I had written a first novel, *The Pillar of Salt*, a life story which was in a sense a trial balloon to help me find the direction of my own life. However, it became clear to me that a real life for a cultured man was impossible in North Africa at that time. I then tried to find another solution, this time through the problems of a mixed marriage, but this second novel, *Strangers*, also led me nowhere. My hopes then rested on the "couple," which still seems to me the most solid happiness of man and perhaps the only real answer to solitude. But I discovered that the couple is not an isolated entity, a forgotten oasis of light in the middle of the world; on the contrary, the whole world is within the couple. For my unfortunate protagonists, the world was that of colonization. I felt that to understand the failure of their undertaking, that of a mixed marriage in a colony, I first had to understand the colonizer and the colonized, perhaps the entire colonial relationship and situation. All this was leading me far from myself and from my own problems, but their explanation became more and more complex; so without knowing where I would end up, I had to at least try to put an end to my own anguish.

It would be equally untrue to say that my ambition in painting this portrait of one of the major oppressions of our time was to describe oppressed peoples in general; it was not even my intention to write about all colonized people. I was Tunisian, therefore colonized. I discovered that few aspects of my life and my personality were untouched by this fact. Not only my own thoughts, my passions and my conduct, but also the conduct of others towards me were affected. As a young student arriving at the Sorbonne for the first time, certain rumors disturbed me. As a Tunisian, would I be allowed to sit for the examinations in philosophy? I went to see the president of the jury. "It is not a right," he explained. "It is a hope." He hesitated, a lawyer looking for the exact words. "Let us say that it is a colonial hope." I have yet to understand what that meant in fact, but I was unable to get anything more out of him. It can be imagined with what serenity I worked after that.

Thus, I undertook this inventory of conditions of colonized people mainly in order to understand myself and to identify my place in the society of other men. It was my readers—not all of them Tunisian—who later convinced me that this portrait was equally theirs. My travels and conversations, meetings and books convinced me, as I advanced in my work on the book, that what I was describing was the fate of a vast multitude across the world. As I discovered that all colonized people have much in common, I was led to the conclusion that all the oppressed are alike in some ways. Nonetheless, while I was writing this book, I preferred to ignore these conclusions that today I maintain are undeniable. So many different persons saw themselves in this portrait that it became impossible to pretend that it was mine alone, or only that of colonized Tunisians, or even North Africans. I was told that in many parts of the world the colonial police confiscated the book in the cells of militant nationalists. I am convinced that I gave them nothing they did not already know, had not already experienced; but as they recognized their own emotions, their revolt, their aspirations, I suppose they appeared more legitimate to them. Above all, whatever the truthfulness of this description of our common experience, it struck them less than the coherence of ideas which I put forward. When the Algerian war was about to break out, I predicted first to myself and then to others the probable dynamism of events. The colonial relationship which I had tried to define chained the colonizer and the colonized into an implacable dependence, molded their respective characters and dictated their conduct. Just as there was an obvious logic in the reciprocal behavior of the two colonial partners, another mechanism, proceeding from the first, would lead, I believed, inexorably to the decomposition of this dependence. Events in Algeria confirmed my hypothesis; I have often verified it since then in the explosion of other colonial situations.

The sum of events through which I had lived since childhood, often incoherent and contradictory on the surface, began to fall into dynamic patterns. How could the colonizer look after his workers while periodically gunning down a crowd of the colonized? How could the colonized deny himself so cruelly yet make such excessive demands? How could he hate the colonizers and yet admire them so passionately? (I too felt this admiration in spite of myself.) I needed to put some sort of order into the chaos of my feelings and to form a basis for my future actions. By temperament and education I had to do this in a disciplined manner, following the conquences as far as possible. If I had not gone all the way, trying to find coherence in all these diverse facts, reconstructing them into portraits which were answerable to one another, I could not have convinced myself and would have remained dissatisfied with my effort. I saw, then, what help to fighting men the simple, ordered description of their misery and humiliation could be. I saw how explosive the objective revelation to the colonized and the colonizer of an essentially explosive condition could be. It was

THE COLONIZED

as if the unveiling of the fatality of their respective paths made the struggle the more necessary and the delaying action the more desperate. Thus, the book escaped from my control.

I must admit I was a bit frightened of it myself. It was clear that the book would be utilized by well-defined colonized people—Algerians, Moroccans, African Negroes. But other peoples, subjugated in other ways—certain South Americans, Japanese and American Negroes—interpreted and used the book. The most recent to find a similarity to their own form of alienation have been the French Canadians. I looked with astonishment on all this, much as a father, with a mixture of pride and apprehension, watches his son achieve a scandalous and applauded fame. Nor was all this uproar totally beneficial, for certain parts of the book of great importance to me were obscured—such as my analysis of what I call the Nero complex; and that of the failure of the European left in general and the Communist Party in particular, for having underestimated the national aspect of colonial liberation; and, above all, the importance, the richness, of personal experience. For I continue to think, in spite of everything, that the importance of this endeavor is its modesty and initial particularity. Nothing in the text is invented or supposed or even hazardously transposed. Actual experience, co-ordinated and stylized, lies behind every sentence. If in the end I have consented to a general tone, it is because I know that I could, at every line, every word, produce innumerable concrete facts.

I have been criticized for not having constructed my portraits entirely around an economic structure, but I feel I have repeated often enough that the idea of privilege is at the heart of the colonial relationship—and that privilege is undoubtedly economic. Let me take this opportunity to reaffirm my position: for me the economic aspect of colonialism is fundamental. The book itself opens with a denunciation of the so-called moral or cultural mission of colonization and shows that the profit motive in it is basic. I have often noted that the *deprivations* of the

On the Colonizer and the Colonized

colonized are the almost direct result of the advantages secured
to the colonizer. However, colonial privilege is not solely economic. To observe the life of the colonizer and the colonized
is to discover rapidly that the daily humiliation of the colonized,
his objective subjugation, is not merely economic. Even the
poorest colonizer thought himself to be—and actually was—
superior to the colonized. This too was part of colonial privilege. The Marxist discovery of the importance of the economy
in all oppressive relationships is not to the point. This relationship has other characteristics which I believe I have discovered
in the colonial relationship. But, one might ask, in the *final
analysis*, don't these phenomena have a more or less hidden
economic aspect? Isn't the motivating force of colonization
economic? The answer is maybe—not certainly. We don't actually know what man is, or just what is essential to him;
whether it is money or sex or pride. . . . Does psychoanalysis
win out over Marxism? Does all depend on the individual or
on society? In any case, before attacking this *final analysis* I
wanted to show all the real complexities in the lives of the
colonizer and the colonized. Psychoanalysis or Marxism must
not, under the pretext of having discovered the source or one of
the main sources of human conduct, pre-empt all experience,
all feeling, all suffering, all the byways of human behavior, and
call them profit motive or Oedipus complex.

I put forward another example which will probably go
against my cause; but I believe that as a writer I must state
everything, even that which can be used against me. My portrait of the colonized, which is very much my own, is preceded
by a portrait of the colonizer. How could I have permitted
myself, with all my concern about personal experience, to draw
a portrait of the adversary? Here is a confession I have never
made before: I know the colonizer from the inside almost as
well as I know the colonized. But I must explain: I said that I
was a Tunisian national. Like all other Tunisians I was treated
as a second-class citizen, deprived of political rights, refused

THE COLONIZED

admission to most civil service departments, etc. But I was not a Moslem. In a country where so many groups, each jealous of its own physiognomy, lived side by side, this was of considerable importance. The Jewish population identified as much with the colonizers as with the colonized. They were undeniably "natives," as they were then called, as near as possible to the Moslems in poverty, language, sensibilities, customs, taste in music, odors and cooking. However, unlike the Moslems, they passionately endeavored to identify themselves with the French. To them the West was the paragon of all civilization, all culture. The Jew turned his back happily on the East. He chose the French language, dressed in the Italian style and joyfully adopted every idiosyncrasy of the Europeans. (This, by the way, is what all colonized try to do before they pass on to the stage of revolt.) For better or for worse, the Jew found himself one small notch above the Moslem on the pyramid which is the basis of all colonial societies. His privileges were laughable, but they were enough to make him proud and to make him hope that he was not part of the mass of Moslems which constituted the base of the pyramid. It was enough to make him feel endangered when the structure began to crumble. The Jews bore arms side by side with the French in the streets of Algiers. My own relations with my fellow Jews were not made any easier when I decided to join the colonized, but it was necessary for me to denounce colonialism, even though it was not as hard on the Jews as it was on the others. Because of this ambivalence I knew only too well the contradictory emotions which swayed their lives. Didn't my own heart beat faster at the sight of the little flag on the stern of the ships that joined Tunis to Marseille?

All this explains why the portrait of the colonizer was in part my own—projected in a geometric sense. My model for the portrait of the colonizer of good will was taken in particular from a group of philosophy professors in Tunis. Their generosity was unquestionable; so, unfortunately, was their impotence, their inability to make themselves heard by anyone else in the colony. However, it was among these men that I felt most at ease. While I was virtuously busy debunking the myths of colonization, could I complacently approve of the counter-myths fabricated by the colonized? I could but smile with my friends at their halting assurance that Andalusian music is the most beautiful in the world; or that Europeans are fundamentally bad (the proof being that they are too harsh with their children). Naturally the result was suspicion on the part of the colonized. And this in spite of the immense good will of this type of French colonizer and the fact that these Frenchmen were already despised by the rest of the French community. I understood only too well their difficulties, their inevitable ambiguity and the resulting isolation; more serious still, their inability to act. All this was a part of my own fate.

Shall I go even further? Though I could not approve of them, I understood even the hard-core colonizers (*pieds noirs*)—they were more simple in thought and action. As I have stated repeatedly, a man is a product of his objective situation; thus I had to ask myself if I would have condemned colonization so vigorously if I had actually benefited from it myself. I hope so, but to have suffered from it only slightly less than the others did has made me more understanding. The most blindly stubborn *pied noir* was, in effect, my born brother. Life has treated us differently; he was the legitimate son of France, heir to privileges which he would defend at any price whatsoever; I was a sort of half-breed of colonization, understanding everyone because I belonged completely to no one.

This book has caused as much anguish and anger as it has enthusiasm. On the one hand, people saw it as an insolent provocation; on the other, a flag to which to rally. Everyone agreed on its militant aspect. It seemed to be an arm in the war against colonization, and indeed it has become one. But nothing seems more ridiculous to me than to boast of borrowed courage and feats never accomplished. I have mentioned how relatively naïve I was when I wrote this book. Then I simply wanted to understand the colonial relationship to which I was bound. I am not saying that my philosophy was alien to my search, my anger and, in a way, my whole life. I am unconditionally opposed to all forms of oppression. For me, oppression is the greatest calamity of humanity. It diverts and pollutes the best energies of man—of oppressed and oppressor alike. For if colonization destroys the colonized, it also rots the colonizer. Be that as it may, provocation was not the object of my work. The effectiveness of the material came gratuitously by the sole virtue of truth.

It was probably sufficient to describe with precision the facts of colonization, the manner in which the colonizer was bound to act, the slow and inevitable destruction of the colonized, to bring to light the absolute iniquity of colonization; and, at the same time, to unveil the fundamental instability of it and predict its demise. My only merit was to have endeavored, over and above my own uneasiness, to describe an unbearable, therefore unacceptable, aspect of reality, one which was destined to provoke continuing upheavals, costly for everyone. Instead of reading this book for its scandalous content or as a permanent provocation to revolt, I hope the reader will calmly examine why these conclusions were reached, conclusions which continue to be reached spontaneously by so many people in similar situations. Is this not simply because these two portraits are faithful to their models? They don't have to recognize themselves in my mirror to discover all by themselves the most useful course of action in their lives of misery. Everyone knows the confusion which still exists between the artist and his subject. Instead of being irritated by what writers say, and accusing them of trying to create disturbances which they only describe and announce, it would be better to listen more attentively and take their warnings more seriously. Do I not have the right, after so many disastrous and useless colonial wars, to think that this book could have been useful to the colonizer as well as to the colonized?

(Translated by Howard Greenfeld)

(Published in the magazine *Arguments* in November, 1958.)

5

The Colonial Problem
and the Left

The "noble" metropolitan

It has become a commonplace to say that the left-wing parties as a whole are perplexed by the colonial problem. Explanations of this are not so readily given, however.

I have shown that the difficulties experienced by *a left-wing colonizer* were the result of a rupture, or a failure to match his ideology to his first-hand experience of the colonial reality.[1]

The left-wing metropolitan had on the whole only ideological opinions, never put to the test in a concrete sense: that is, by direct contact with colonization or colonized peoples. For this reason *the left-wing metropolitan* was apparently more consistent and more assured in his opinions than *the left-wing colonizer*. He also had a more generous approach and took a more abstract view of things. Thus, the victims of colonization conceived the myth of the *Frenchman of France* or the "noble" metropolitan, who was better, more understanding and more impartial than their colonizers.

Hence also the feeling, in the mind of the colonizer, that the metropolitan really understood nothing about colonization.

[1] See *The Colonizer and the Colonized,* in particular: Ch. 2, 1st part.

The Colonial Problem and the Left

The *Francaouis,* as they were called among the colonizers, were stupid, irritating and politically dangerous, because of their irresponsible attitude.

Then came the war in Indochina, events in Tunisia and in Morocco, and particularly the Algerian war; gradually the real state of affairs was brought home to those in France; inexorably the metropolitan and his ideology were brought face to face with the reality, in a confrontation that became daily more and more painful.

Like all those in the home country, the left-wing metropolitan who has witnessed these historic events finds his opinions necessarily being modified, even, in some cases, violently upset. This time he is obliged to choose and to make decisions which are often painful for him.

The "noble" colonized

The left-wing metropolitan's opinion of colonialism, before the above-mentioned events, should clearly be examined within the context of his whole political attitude.

In theory, if not always in actual fact, the left-wing metropolitan showed a tendency towards a universal humanism, of a social and secular kind, though it was universal, secular and social to varying degrees. There were those who were nationalists at heart, though their opinions were tinged with universalism (like the radicals); there were those whose sympathies were international, though they were prone to attacks of nationalism (like the communist workers), etc. . . . But on the whole this was how the left-wing metropolitan saw himself.

His view of the colonized formed an integral part of this picture: he desired the welfare of all colonized peoples, and, in a way, their liberation. But the liberation he envisaged for them was essentially a social one. He also wanted to further their cultural and spiritual progress, though this desire was often less clearly felt. In short, he would have liked the colonized to enjoy the same privileges he sought for himself. For the class struggle was paramount in his eyes: and he had, moreover, already come to grips with cultural problems. If he also admitted that the question of freedom for colonized peoples was on a *national* level, he insisted at the same time that this national liberation should go hand in hand with social liberation, for him the *sine qua non* of the whole adventure. On the basis of his reasoning for himself in terms of *class,* he infers what is good for the colonized.

The metropolitan's concern for the fate of colonized peoples depends at once *on the particular view he holds of himself and on his conception of the nature and requirements of colonized man.*

I could attempt an inventory of this conception of the colonized *before the colonial crises;* I shall instead restrict myself to observing that since the metropolitan did not directly dominate the colonized, he had no experience of the negative aspects of colonial relations, which play such an important part in our understanding of left-wing colonizers. Even if the presence of this domination had been *demonstrated* to him, together with the fact that it had important consequences, one of which for instance was that the metropolitan himself reaped considerable advantages from it, and that he too stood in a certain *relation to the colony,* this relation still remained something *abstract* for him, lacking the *reality* of an experience.

Brief encounter

So, as we have shown, a new situation arose from the collapse of the French colonial empire: the residents of the mother country found themselves abruptly face to face with the colonial reality. It is not surprising that their various myths were in danger of being destroyed . . . and perhaps of being replaced by others. It is hard to live with a threatening reality,

The Colonial Problem and the Left

and so men have invented myths by which they can escape it.

We must find out how this confrontation occurred, and, first of all, we must describe the nature of the different movements for colonial liberation.

As I have demonstrated elsewhere, these of necessity assumed an essentially *national, nationalistic, a-social, political and religious form.* If the social aspect was at all in evidence, it never took first place, and in many cases, was even rejected completely. The political aspect was by far the most important, often in a bad way. And the religious element was often used, if only as a pretext.

Understandably this was already sufficient *to disturb the ideology of left-wing metropolitans:* they had always been suspicious of nationalistic demands, which they considered as a convenient disguise for class interests. Now they could no longer entertain such an idea, since these demands clearly had *no class bias.* The same was true for the religious aspect.

Their perplexity would, I think, have remained on an ideological level *had there been no material basis for left-wing hesitations.*

This is of capital importance. The French left wing represents and defends the interests of the French masses. At least this is the role in which it sees itself; and it is for the most part true. So we must observe how the masses reacted when brought face to face for the first time with the colonized. Or in other words, to use a well-known phraseology: what is the new infrastructure of left-wing ideology with regard to colonization?

On the whole the answer is that the French people reacted in a negative way.[1] Rightly or wrongly, they believed them-

[1] By and large, here is what happened: *the majority of Frenchmen ended by taking from the left all power of action.* They entrusted to General de Gaulle the task of resolving their colonial difficulties.

selves victimized when the colonies were abandoned. Xenophobia was a characteristic feature of their reaction (which
even the most pro-French foreigners could not deny). The
more they saw of the colonized, the more they *rejected* them. It
would be worth making a more thorough analysis of this re-
vival of xenophobia. But keeping strictly to the metropolitan
attitude to the colonized, let us merely note: the presence of a
large number of Algerians in France, very much members of
the proletariat, and as such inspiring contempt in a rich people;
various disastrous experiences; a war which affected everyone
to different degrees; fear; humiliation; feelings of guilt because
of complicity in torture, etc. And of course, we must not forget
that a lot of sanctimonious hypocrites did everything they
could to make matters worse.

In conclusion, to use a figure of speech, we may say that
when it was put to the test of reality, *the myth of the "noble"
metropolitan simply dissolved.* It was replaced in the minds of
the colonized by the idea that the Frenchman of France no
longer existed, or even that he had ever existed; and by a tendency to lump all Frenchmen together in the same category,
which was just as false.

On the other hand, *the myth of the "noble" colonized was
also destroyed,* and we shall see later what replaced this.

So the meeting between the "noble" metropolitan and the
"noble" colonized blew both those figments of the imagination

---

No matter how often we exclaim: they were wrong, they were mistaken, they were deceived . . . we are criticizing their decision, we are
at most trying to explain it, but the *fact* itself still remains. The French
decided that it would be better to take the matter out of the hands of
the Left Wing, including the liberals. And quite frankly, were they
wrong? At the risk of shocking my left-wing friends, I must speak plainly
here. Though it may give an occasional twitch, de Gaulle has finally
laid the ghost of the French colonial empire, and he will go down in
history for it. Some will say, and I think they are right, that decolonization would have taken its course in any case. Nevertheless, it was he
who wound up the process. Why was the Left Wing not capable of
taking on the job?

sky-high. After this, as I demonstrated with the colonizer and the colonized, neither subject could ever be quite the same again.

How the French left reacted

At first it was thrown right off balance. If its opinions had been shaken by the demands of the colonized, they were shattered by the reaction of the masses in France, for whom, let us not forget, the left is the self-elected spokesman and agent. The left had lost its bearings, both in terms of left-wing politics and of French politics.

On the level of left-wing politics the left did not find among the colonized the structures it thought to see in them; nor, which is more serious still, what it was fighting for, its very *raison d'être*. On the other hand, it felt itself abandoned by its own followers: their reaction did not correspond to its ideals.

As a French group it was no good trying to avoid the issue, or even to deny it: the left was involved on a national level. The colonized were a nation making demands on another nation; and the left's adherents were reacting in a genuinely national way.

The left was to fall victim to a paralysis, progressively more and more acute. Here, in passing, we might refute a common objection: if the left was brought to a standstill, it was simply because it had no concerted plan of action.[1] I believe that the trouble is unfortunately more deep-seated and serious than that. The left had no concerted plan of action, because it had no common *political program*, and that again because by now it hardly has a common *doctrine*.

The result of this deficiency was that the left split over this problem. For the left to pass resolutions, if any, it had to undergo a splintering, even within one and the same group, and

[1] This argument still holds good today for many other problems. Unity of action is impossible without a common creed.

even within each single individual. The diversity of political positions allows every kind of interest, according to each individual concern, and to satisfy all people's desires, since under cover of such confusion anything may be upheld. Worse still, in each attitude one can discern a trace of all the others. Having said this much, it is possible roughly to distinguish a nationalist reaction; an attitude of unconditional support for the victims of colonization; and opportunism.

To understand this, beyond the context of this particular crisis, we must take into account the ideological history of each group, the present state of its political components, and the relations of these components to the rest—i.e., the overall political scene.

The nationalist reaction and the gloomy myth of the colonized

This is the simplest and the most naïve reaction, fostered by grievances and by fear. So, that's how it is! So these colonized people turn out to be greedy, aggressive, blood-thirsty fanatics; "after all we have done for them" they are just ungrateful nationalists. When we had already grown out of nationalism (or thought we had). Well then, we will be as nationalistic as they are; and since they are making war on us, we will reply in kind.

This was the kind of bemused reaction, growing steadily more irritated until it burst into anger, to be found in many socialist teachers. It is a reactionary attitude, to be sure, but in a way it shows a clear conscience and the claims it makes are ethical; they are those of a secular humanist bewildered by events, of a universalist who feels himself cheated and who, in a certain sense, has been. Socialist teachers had sincerely believed that sooner or later, with patience, time, the help of a non-religious republican education and the reforms obtained

The Colonial Problem and the Left

by the socialist party, a great worldwide fraternity would be
born, to flourish chiefly between colonizer and colonized. Even
when this view seemed most sorely tried, it had a certain attraction; it was naïve perhaps, with a positively grammar
school naïveté, but at least it was broad-minded and resolutely
anti-racist, for example. Unfortunately, as a result, the awaken-
ing was all the more rude. The demands of the colonized
looked so oddly like what the socialists were fighting against,
that they could not but treat them as suspect.

*It is easy to see how they were led to re-open the case for
colonization, this time on appeal.* They were uncertain whether
the victims of colonization, who were now displaying such
blind ingratitude and such faithlessness, had ever really been
victims. Embarked on this slippery course, as the war continued, with one grievance giving rise to the next, and ideological
contamination rife, they were compelled to revise one by one
all the "whereases" of this lawsuit that had seemed so finally ripe
for judgment, until, to the amazement of the socialists themselves, everything seemed uncertain once more.

We cannot at this point go into the arguments put forward
by these unexpected prosecutors of the colonized—in the name
of socialist morality—but they can be found in the series *La
Revue Socialiste,* where the violence of feeling expressed
against the colonized often exceeds that of right-wing periodicals.

Let us merely observe that the same process is to be found
here that I have already studied in *The Colonizer and the Colonized;* that is to say, an essential *denigration of the colonized.*
Bit by bit, the left-wing metropolitans who react nationalisti-
cally begin to see the colonized through the eyes of the ordi-
nary colonialist: as a fanatic and backward people, incapable
of self-government, hypocritical, brutal, etc., etc. Little by
little, as the sociologist Edgar Morin laughingly pointed out to
me, the "Noble Savage" becomes the "Unspeakable Papuan."

THE COLONIZED

By whatever means they arrive at this attitude, and whatever the blend of sentiments that lies behind it, it is clearly one of ridiculous confusion, resulting in the following:

Bewilderment, and gradual submission to "national" objectives on the part of the Left, to such an extent that the left wing *as such* fades out completely.

Contradiction: starting as universal humanists, they end up as chauvinists involved in colonial warfare . . . while still posing as the advocates of peace and the liberation of all peoples.

Futility: it would not matter if by these means the left managed to solve the problem; but in fact *the right can always outbid the left on this score.*

Dishonor: in the eyes of the colonized, in the eyes of the world and even in the eyes of the socialists themselves; for the left is often humiliated also in the eyes of many of its own adherents.

In short, *the left disqualifies itself from the fight, and commits a fruitless suicide.*

Unconditional support, or "the colonized are always right"

The final justifications produced by members of the "new left" and by so-called progressive Christians are different. It is interesting to note, however, that they have often joined forces on political issues.

By and large both parties say this: colonized people are what they are, and they must be accepted as they are. Their cause is just, the rest is incidental and superficial.

The result of this *petitio principii* is roughly as follows:

It is not our concern: we have no right to judge them. We should not interfere with them in their struggle, even if we do not approve of certain of the initiatives they take. (ex. Sartre: *Les Temps Modernes.*)

It is interesting to see that the followers of these two groups,

The Colonial Problem and the Left

men of the greatest possible honesty and the most staunch adherents of the left, show a high proportion of intellectuals
among their ranks; of people, too, whose political moral sense
has not been overlaid by overly compelling personal interests.

Progressive Christians support the colonized more wholeheartedly than anyone else; with such enthusiasm, in fact, that
the result is curious. They have no apparent policy, and they
are not in the least self-conscious: their motives seem to belong
on another plane—I almost said to another world. On this
theme, I recall a delightful *bon mot* of Claude Roy's: "Since the
Christians cannot convert the Muslims to Christianity, they are
now trying to convert them to Islam."

I think it is here that we can find the explanation of the extraordinary about face of Christians on the colonial problem.
The motives animating progressive Christians are not exactly
those of the left: it just happens that by a twist of historical fate
they fit in with left-wing politics. But the basic problem is to
find a new line of Christian political action with regard to the
ex-, or future ex-colonies, which will save Christianity in those
countries, or at least keep the way open for it. I hasten to add
that a large measure of generosity, courage and devotion accompanies these plans; and also that, as all Christians do not
see eye to eye in this affair, the progressive Christians are often
heavily penalized.

This attitude, apparently the most assured, and most faithful
to left-wing ideals, has also proved hard to maintain. The trouble is—we must repeat it once again—that, in this case too,
those concerned have refused to examine the new, unexpected
reality for which their ideology has left them unprepared. Instead of confronting it squarely, they distort it—or rather, for
reality is indifferent to our concerns—they distort their own
perception of it. In other words, *they create a new myth*: the
myth of the civilized colonized who is always right, and who
needs nothing.

We can soon see that by adopting this attitude they abandon

THE COLONIZED

both the universal and the international front, whereas they were making—or thought they were making—every effort to maintain that position. For, in the long run no true internationalist can say: this does not concern me. He cannot accept the sacrifice of his personal interests and consent to look beyond the limits of his own circle, if he is not concerned to further the welfare of others. The left voted for intervention in Spain precisely because it believed such to be its business. International organizations, whether political or trade-unionist, exist for this purpose.

It is impossible not to see that such an attitude on a tactical level leads to the toleration of every kind of excess—terrorism, xenophobia, social reaction, etc.

This is exactly what has happened. It is impossible to overemphasize the fact that by this attitude the left-wing intellectuals, among others, *have done little to help the colonized to define his position.* On the contrary, they have fostered in him every kind of mental and spiritual disorder, and have added to the perplexity of those few victims of colonization who had retained a relatively sharp and morally sound political sense. A colonized intellectual must find it hard, for instance, to condemn terrorism, if non-colonized intellectuals are so lukewarm in their attack on it. He will have difficulty too in censuring the exploitation of religion, if they find it quite natural.

The purely tactical approach leaves unresolved the problem of what to do with *non-colonized people living in a colony* (or an ex-colony). Now these people do exist, and they are not always to blame for the situation. Even if they were, one cannot ignore the fate of whole groups of human beings simply because they are not at that particular moment suffering oppression. At any rate, that is no way for a universalist to behave.

Considering the problem from this angle, it is difficult to see why the mother country should continue to help the colonized, especially after their revolt and liberation. It is clear, however, that the colonized need everything, technical as well as cultural aid. Left-wing metropolitans today then find themselves up against another contradiction: *on the one hand they have consented to a total separation of colonizer from colonized, but on the other hand they discover that the colonized need outside aid.*

They rescue themselves from the dilemma by saying vaguely that they must *make it up to them.* Are there really many political programs founded solely on moral obligations?

In fact, the colonized that have been ignored by history, largely because of their subjection to colonization, must now be reinstated in an international context and approached in a genuine attempt at international solidarity. It is not possible to change over from *colonization to nothing;* the move must be from colonization to a kind of world-wide organization, where everyone has the right—yes, the right—to concern himself with the affairs of the rest.

To sum up, it may be that we have a paradox here: highly suspicious at the outset of any nationalistic reflex, the left-wing unconditional supporter ends oddly enough by endorsing the nationalism of the colony, and, in consequence, taking up an "everyone for himself" attitude. So, almost without realizing it we come full circle back to nationalism.

Opportunism

Communist opportunism is one of the most surprising results of the whole affair. I think the communists' difficulties may be summed up in a sentence I have already used elsewhere: "The hour of national liberation of the colonized has come earlier than the hour of world revolution."

Now, for the communists—as for most socialists—the only true freedom is that achieved by revolution. They are uncertain of this other kind, in which there is an element of the unexpected, and so something obscure and disturbing. (Incidentally, this is, from an *objective* point of view, perhaps unfortunate: the socialist revolution might have enabled the colonized to skip the nationalist stage—perhaps; but it is not certain. If there had been a "Union of the Democratic Republicans of France and Africa," the confusion in the minds of left-wing ideologists would have been less serious. The left might, with a clear conscience, have demanded the retention of the ex-colonies in the Union.)

At all events, despite Stalin's book, and despite the few passages in Lenin's works on the question of nationalism, the communists can never consider the national liberation of the colonized as anything other than a substitute for that other liberation, as any more than one lap of the journey.

The story of the evolution of communist opinion is one of acute embarrassment. Having put up a fight against the first manifestations of national feeling, because they underestimated their strength and because they hoped that the socialist revolution would take place before the nationalists could achieve their goal (witness 1936), they decided to give some ground, always with the intention of saving the day in the long run.

In this case it was an attempt to arrange the future to their liking: first by winning the confidence of the nationalists, since it was they who had the confidence of the rank and file in the colony, since it was their words that were listened to and their ideas that carried weight; and at the same time by refusing to break the links that bound colonial subjects to the mother country. Basically *they still believe that the revolution would come from the mother country.* They did not even have any real confidence in the local communist parties, probably still controlled from the metropolis.

There is another reason, apparently quite a different one, for their behavior, which nevertheless links up with the foregoing: this is, the influence of Russian policy (another phrase could be substituted without altering the basic meaning: so we might

The Colonial Problem and the Left

say "Russian advice," "the interests of the U.S.S.R." or "the exigencies of world-wide revolution"). The efforts of the colonized country to free itself are often nationalistic, making it turn towards America, or in other words, towards a bourgeois society, for help. The peculiar combination of economic and historical circumstances often makes this necessary (U.N., military and economic aid, etc. . . .). Thus Russia can scarcely avoid being suspicious of these efforts. Moreover, if the colonized nation begins to vacillate between two forms of imperialism, the dying French and the strong, healthy American, better guide them towards the decadent one. (Quite possibly behind this lies the hope that France will be worn out by the struggle, and N.A.T.O. thereby weakened.)

Here once more we are faced with a contradictory political situation. On the one hand the party approves colonial liberation because it is in step with the march of civilization; on the other hand this liberation masquerades in a highly suspicious guise, and has escaped the control both of French revolutionaries and of the U.S.S.R. (recent Russian influence over Egypt and the U.A.R. requires separate analysis).

As a result communist activity was also quite obviously inconsistent and at odds with itself; so much so that the Party underwent slow paralysis where colonial problems were concerned. Some militant communists were killed fighting in Algeria, while others were tortured because of anti-military activity. The French communist party proclaimed its indignation, and voted full powers to the governments conducting the war; they would have gone even farther if by so doing they could have strengthened their alliance with the socialists, for example, for they were still sure that this was the most important and the most urgent thing. After a while communist activity ceased altogether, and complete paralysis or political unreality ensued.

Here too we must, of course, take into account the role played by communist sympathizers. If all these had been reso-

THE COLONIZED

lutely against the war, that would surely have given the communists pause. But it can be definitely asserted that their supporters, particularly among the working classes, aided and abetted them in such conduct. When at last communist workers resigned themselves to the loss of Algeria, it was through indifference, weariness and disgust, not because the ethics of revolution demanded it, nor out of sympathy for the North Africans. Quite the contrary: their fear of foreigners, a new kind of anger against the North Africans, anxiety in case their own standard of living were to suffer, etc. . . . All these assumed dangerous proportions, fed by propaganda in the movies, the radio and the press. It was not, then, entirely the communists' fault; they were wrong, however, in so far as *they confirmed their followers in this state of mind.* They made no sort of serious stand against the propaganda, and did nothing to dissipate this growing foreigner-hatred in the minds of their workers, nor to show them that neither socialism, nor perhaps their own primary interests, could find satisfaction in the colonial wars. But to do that they would first have had to be convinced of it themselves.

Liberal opportunism

I really do not know whether it is still correct to speak of the left; the term is, however, commonly accepted for purposes of classification. After all, the socialists have swung so far in the opposite direction that it is not difficult to be more left than they.

I think the root of the matter, for the liberals, lies in safeguarding French economic interests in the colonies, or in the ex-colonies. For certain intelligent "young heads of firms," a liberal policy, the economic welfare of the country and their own private interests happen to coincide.

This is not absurd, at least from a French point of view. It is probable that the French middle classes committed a grave historical error by putting Mendès-France out of action. For he might well have saved something vital: our economic links with the colonies, while granting them administrative autonomy.

But, of course, it was not certain, and there was some risk involved (which they refused to run, preferring the risk of losing everything).

The *arrangement* proposed by the liberals, Mendès-France among them, would possibly not last long. The energy of the colonized in their struggle for freedom, though it might be reined in for a moment by these agreements, could break out again, escaping the control of the native bourgeoisie, who had signed the pacts. Quite frankly I believe, and at the time I told Mendès-France what I thought, that this is what would have happened sooner or later.

The members of the colony were still the injured parties; and after some hesitation *they returned to the attack.*

French civil servants, who form a large part of the colonizers in a colony, realized that their situation was hopeless. *They were the most virulent in their attacks on Mendès-France,* and had no difficulty in finding others, in Paris, to defend them (opposition from the civil service was, to everyone's astonishment, greater than from colonists).

Whatever the rights and wrongs of the case, liberal opportunism, whether possible or not in theory, failed in practice. This policy could not save the day either.

To sum up briefly: when the left actually came into contact with the victims of colonization as real human beings, and with colonization as a real sociological and political fact; that is, when they witnessed the way *in which colonial subjects set about obtaining their freedom;* and *in which the masses in France reacted to the demands of the above;* there resulted *ideological turmoil* in the very center of the French left and *action, or rather a failure to take action,* which led the left to

THE COLONIZED

disqualify itself, since it joined forces with the right, although by so doing it did not even increase its power of action; or *contradict itself* as a left-wing group; or *resign* and succumb to a kind of *sclerosis;* it led in all three cases to impotence and self-negation.[1]

The remedy

I should like to return now to a methodological distinction which I drafted all too rapidly in *The Colonizer and the Colonized:* that between desired and observed reality.

I said that it was necessary to separate these two stages clearly one from another: that we had first *to get a discussion going with an inventory of the pros and cons of the situation, and only look into* the possibility of a solution *afterwards.* An observation may be perfectly correct, whereas desires may be highly debatable, for this reason, among others, that observation concerns what is real, whereas wishes belong to the realm of hypothesis, of the future, and often of ethics, or simply of sentiment. If we are over-concerned with solutions we shall hinder and obscure our study of observable fact.

[1] Already in that particular issue of *Arguments,* and often since then, I have had interminable discussions with my left-wing friends. With the lapse of time, people begin to forget how they behaved in particular circumstances, or, if they do remember, they invent for their actions the motives which best suit them now. No Christian has ever yet given me a satisfactory explanation of the complete volte-face of the Church over the colonial problem. Not one of them, as far as I know, has ever taken exception to my explanations. The communists, as usual, call on the authorities: to the analysis of the facts and their different attitudes to them, they oppose the *writings* of Stalin, Lenin, etc. . . . Yes or no, did the communists vote full powers for the escalation of the war? Yes or no, did they not discourage the young men of the contingent? Yes or no, did they not cut themselves off from the Moslem proletariat in North Africa, by attacking their national leaders? If we cannot begin by admitting that at the least the left wing made mistakes in colonial politics, we shall never be able to debate the question, nor draw any useful lessons for the future.

The Colonial Problem and the Left

I have tried here to analyze the sociological, psychological, and political circumstances of the French left with regard to the colonial problem, and to offer an explanation of their ideological confusion and their inability to act.

I should prefer it if these suggestions were debated on their own merits, leaving aside for the time being the "remedies."

Having made this clear, I think I may be allowed, by way of an addendum, to ask just one question: what can the left do to extricate itself from the situation?

I believe for my part that it must *retrieve its identity*.

To understand what this means we ought to re-define exactly what it signifies to belong to the left, and to recall the basic tenets of the left's political philosophy and system of ethics. Sooner or later this is going to be necessary. In the meanwhile, I offer one or two suggestions, which seem to me appropriate to our subject.

The left must reassert its universalism in word and deed; far from thinking that they have failed, or that present needs oblige them to postpone this reassertion for a while.

This means, as far as we are concerned, that they must never re-open the case for colonization; it is definitively closed. Or, at any rate, if any particular detail or point of view seems in need of correction, they must still take as their basic assumption the absolute necessity of emancipation for the colonies, and not make the usual mental reservations (e.g. cultural paternalism: "Oh, no! Not culture!"). At the same time they must stop saying: it is not our affair. It *is* our affair, since we belong to the left. And they must not be afraid to assert at the same time that bonds do exist between peoples, that a race has not got a right to unlimited self-determination. It has no right to become in its turn an imperial power or an oppressor; and every minority has the right to be respected for what distinguishes it from the rest, etc. . . .

This will not bring us back to the above-mentioned mental

THE COLONIZED

reservations, because we can say all this so much more easily once we have *unequivocally* affirmed the need for liberation— for a genuine liberation, with no regrets.

This leads us to the problem of nationalism. The left must find the courage to make a definite stand on the subject of nationalism. That is to say that, here again, they must *admit its existence,* without reservations, and not as if they regretted it. They must also stop trying to cheat with nationalism, by leaving the nationalists in the lurch every time, for example, that some other interest comes into play (electoral considerations, Russian or French popular interests, etc.). And they must then make nationalism *an integral part of left-wing views;* instead of letting it stay stuck in their throats like a bone they are always longing to cough up, they might try to digest it, or in other words, to *judge* it.

Nationalism is at present the standard to which many nations (whether colonized or not, in point of fact) rally in their fight for freedom; it is for this reason that it is something genuine and constructive. To reject it is mere abstract intellectualization: the negation of what is real. But, if we accept nationalism without argument and without reflection, we are again disqualifying ourselves. We must judge it and make up our minds about its errors and about the various manifestations which give it a bad name and in the end do it harm, or, more simply, do harm to the lives of other groups of people.

I will give as an example the problem of blind, civilian terrorism. The extent to which the left manages to absorb the nationalism of the colonized, without going back on itself, is precisely what allows it to reject this terrorism—compels it rather. If on the other hand, it hesitates on such fundamental issues, then any pronouncements it makes will look like *calculated policy.*

So we arrive at the problem of policy. It is high time that strategy was put *in its right place.* It is extraordinary, but there

The Colonial Problem and the Left

is scarcely a single publication in Paris that still sets truth before policy.

This is not necessarily a sign of cowardice nor of deliberate self-seeking; far from it, it is rather because *the truth no longer imposes itself upon us with sufficient force;* because it seems to us that a line of policy will have more impact (whether in word or deed: in order to obtain a desired effect, one often acts in an apparently opposite sense).

Over and over again it must be emphasized that policy is not all: it has its own importance, certainly, but must not be allowed to swallow up all other considerations; otherwise it will lead to total negation. Policy, which should be only *a roundabout way* of getting at the truth, and of making its position surer, soon becomes our sole pursuit, and ends by obscuring all other points of view, so that we no longer know ourselves very clearly what our aim is.[1]

[1] I need hardly point out that this passage is intended neither as an accusation, nor as a string of insults aimed at the left and at left-wing intellectuals. It is simply an analysis of a deficiency that I deplore. I should add, though, that I consider the left-wing intellectuals do honor to their country, and that there are not many nations in the world that can boast of having so many generous, brave men of good-will.

(Translated by Jane Brooks)

(A discussion with students of the
Ecole des Hautes Etudes Commerciales, Paris,
published in the school revue, December, 1967.)

6

Are the
French Canadians
Colonized?

Students: Mr. Memmi, two years ago, when you were working on the second edition of your book *The Colonizer and the
Colonized,* you chose to dedicate it to "my friends the French
Canadians . . ." Was it even then your intention to suggest
that, in your opinion, the French Canadians were in a true
sense the victims of colonization?

Albert Memmi: I think it is clear that when I wrote my book
I was not thinking of the French Canadians. But the fact that I
knew a few of them, and that these people had become my
friends, led me to take an interest in their problems—and indeed this interest dates from some time ago. When I had finished my book I had an interview with a French Canadian literary critic, Pierre de Grandpré, which was broadcast on the
Quebec radio. A short while after, I received a letter from a
young Canadian, Hubert Aquin, who was later to become one
of the new School of Montreal writers. He asked me to speak of
my experience of colonization on French Canadian television. I
accepted, of course, though I was surprised that the Canadians
should be interested in colonization. (Unless I am mistaken,

the film was in fact not shown.) I understood why when I noticed that Hubert Aquin constantly pointed out parallels between what I described, and what he felt and thought as a
Canadian. This was the beginning of our discussion and our
correspondence. Later, I was once again to see Pierre de
Grandpré, who, though a moderate, was to confirm for me the
truth of this point of view expressed by many French Canadians. Then I made the acquaintance of the Angry Young Men of
Montreal, the staff of the revue *Parti-Pris.* On another occasion,
d'Allemagne, Vice-President of the R.I.N. (Rassemblement
pour l'Indépendance), on a visit to Paris, asked if he might
meet certain men whom he considered capable of understanding, and then of explaining to the French people, the opinions
of those who advocated independence for his country. We met
at a dinner, at which, as I recall, Jacques Berque and Jean La-
courture were present. D'Allemagne informed me, among other
things, that *The Colonizer and the Colonized* was printed and
circulated secretly in Canada.

I still reserved my judgment, however, until I could check
the facts for myself. Then one day I received an invitation from
Canadian television to go to Quebec. It was thus that I was
able to observe the various different ways in which the Canadians were really dominated, and that this was a source of distress to them.

Students: The French Canadians consider that they have, on
an economic and social level, been colonized by the English
Canadians. What is confusing, however, for French opinion,
and for those Frenchmen who visit Canada, is the prosperity, if
not real at least apparent, of the province of Quebec. It seems
rather that there are two colonizing nations, one of which has
got the upper hand. It is the Indians who are really the colonized race.

Albert Memmi: Two things have perplexed the French (and
the left wing in particular, who have lost another chance of
expressing themselves properly in a case that should be close to

THE COLONIZED

their hearts): the French Canadians' *standard of living*, and the *nationalistic tone* of their protest.

It is certain that the French Canadians' standard of living is on the whole comparatively higher than the Europeans'. It is closer to the Americans', which for Frenchmen today seems the height of luxury. It is also true that the word colonization suggests material and cultural poverty. But this is because we have in mind the African or Asian type of colonization.

I should like at this point to recall two supplementary hypotheses, which I have frequently made use of, and of whose truth I have recently seen evidence in the case of the black Americans. They are that each domination is relative, and each is specific.

It is clear that no one is oppressed in the absolute, but always in relation to someone else, in a given context. In such a way that, even if one is fortunate in comparison with others, or with oneself in another situation, one may perfectly well be living in a state of domination, and suffering all the ills inherent in it, even the most serious. It is so, apparently, with the French Canadians.

But theirs is by no means a unique case. The same is true for the black Americans. When one compares the plight of black Americans, from all points of view, with that of black Africans, again accounting for all its features, it is tempting to say: the black Americans should not complain so, for they, dominated, are far and away richer then the black Africans in their freedom. My American publisher, Howard Greenfeld, has told me that the first time Danilo Dolci, the champion of the Sicilian poor, came to New York, he asked at once to see "the Poor." And when he was taken to Harlem, he grew very angry and would not believe that these great apartment houses were the American equivalent of slums. Yet *relatively speaking*, the blacks of America are dominated by the whites. Everyone knows by now that they are the last to find employment, the

Are the French Canadians Colonized?

first to be fired, that they are subject to a political discrimination, that racism goes very deep, and so on.

For I want to make it clear too, that domination, even though it is relative, can have *absolute* consequences: the domination of the French by the English Canadians also means that the economy is *really* in the hands of the Anglo-Americans, that the labor market is controlled by them, etc. . . . So this is not merely our relative impression. This relativity is a part of the objective condition of the dominating and the dominated race.

Moreover, the economy is not the only thing to be considered. Grievances in the field of culture, for instance, are strong too. Up to now this has always been something of a joke, and we have laughed about the quaint, old-fashioned French spoken by Canadians. And yet . . .

Students: This cultural *malaise* impressed us most particularly. Education is entirely in the hands of the English, even in places where the French minority is at its largest. In New Brunswick, for instance, where 38% of the population is French-speaking, or in Manitoba, where there are still large groups of French people, French is no longer used outside the home. In Quebec the English supremacy is less marked, for Quebec is a powerful province, which levies its own taxes, etc. . . .

Albert Memmi: In Canada, I once again met a version of a phenomenon more or less constantly recurrent in the majority of colonial situations, and which I have termed *colonial bilingualism.* There is an official, working language, that of the ruling class, and a mother tongue, that has little or no currency in the conduct of urban affairs. There is nothing against people speaking two languages, except when the language which they consider the more important is subordinated and stigmatized, as here. This is the difference between colonial bilingualism and bilingualism pure and simple. But as I have spoken of this elsewhere, I shall not press the point now. At all events, here is a situation of the type I have already described, with nearly all

THE COLONIZED

the psychological and social characteristics: the French Canadians are not only embarrassed by their language, they are a little ashamed of it too; and they defend it fiercely. I was present at a most awkward scene that took place in a shop in Montreal, when the young man who was with me took the salesgirl violently to task, because, although a French Canadian herself, she was pretending not to speak French. . . .

A Student: A French Canadian, with whom I was doing a crossword puzzle, said to me: "The dreadful thing is that we don't know how to define our words." On the other hand, they pride themselves on using *"fin de semaine"* instead of "weekend," and *"emmagasinage"* instead of "shopping." They have demanded, and obtained, certain changes in the restaurants, and in some firms, but in contrast advertising is still almost completely a product of the English-speaking community.

Albert Memmi: Only here again, this linguistic, and even cultural, domination, in the widest sense of the term, is not just a piece of picturesque folklore. It reveals itself in the very real results it produces. In business enterprises the English language is compulsory, and those who do not speak it often cannot aspire to a large number of jobs, particularly in higher grade employment. (Naturally the inevitable reaction is now setting in: the young contributors to *Parti-Pris* told me that they refused jobs where they were obliged to know English. They pretend to understand only French.) In many of the provinces it would be impossible to get one's education in French. If one wishes to pursue an administrative career, it is better to be armed with a good knowledge of English. So linguistic deficiency here is not only an ideological or purely cultural problem. A kind of circular movement is set up: economic and political domination gives rise to a cultural subordination, and this cultural subordination in its turn maintains the economic and political sub-domination.

Students: Hence the urgency of the French Canadians' protest about cultural matters, voiced simultaneously with complaints concerning their economic status.

Albert Memmi: That is true. In my opinion it is impossible to overestimate the significance of the birth of a French Canadian literature. To be sure this literature has always existed, but never on so large a scale, nor crowned with such frequent success. I observed the same thing in the case of the North Africans. Without knowing whether their country would ever achieve independence, a certain number of young writers set out to describe their existence as men under domination. They had considerable influence in the outside world, because there was a vague feeling that something was in the air.

Students: Even lyrical pop songs are now involved in the movement in Canada, and enjoying a great success. There is one song called "I am of French Canadian nationality," which tells the epic tale of a man who threw bombs and who has been languishing in prison for the past seven years, because he had at the time dared to do what everyone is thinking today.

Albert Memmi: The same is true of the appearance of periodicals like *Parti-Pris*: nowadays, newspapers are not afraid to be constantly discussing these topics, and a dialogue is being established among the intellectuals, the journalists, the writers and the readers. A dialogue with the outside world as well. This whole cultural reawakening is one of the clearest proofs— if proof were needed—of the new national consciousness of the body of French Canadians. Without taking into account the fact that all this tells us far more about the real state of affairs in Canada, than all the political speeches.

Students: You said that there were two things which perplexed the French. The second was that French Canadian claims take on a *nationalistic* character.

Albert Memmi: To those in Paris, the Canadian outcry for national independence often seems both romantic and reactionary, particularly in the opinion of the left wing. At a time

THE COLONIZED

when everyone is talking of building Europe, when the world is divided into two or three blocs, which draw all the other countries into line with themselves, it is surely difficult to speak any longer of nations, except in jest. That is not untrue of Western Europe, even though there, to take France for example, the question is not as simple as all that. De Gaulle's nationalism satisfies a need still deeply felt in the hearts of the French people; the left wing has either not yet quite grasped this fact, or prefers to ignore it (with the exception of the Communists, who are probably aware of it). They believe, or pretend to believe, that the ruling classes are throwing dust in the eyes of the people; which is false. Nationalism is the expression of a phenomenon still very much alive and relatively deep-rooted; it is perhaps to be deplored, and it is perhaps a stage we have to grow out of, but that is a different consideration. We must first acknowledge its existence and analyze it correctly. At any rate, in the case of colonized countries, it is a fact that most claims are made on a national basis. It is possible that the claimants are in the wrong, but no one can condemn (and above all, no one can deny) a reality in the name of the preconceived idea they had of it. I am fairly sure that scholasticism was a product of that kind of mentality. It is much more intelligent to analyze why things happen in this way. The jibes and sarcasms of the Paris newspapers—and even their stringency—with regard to the Canadians' national aspirations I must admit I found exasperating. As, in fact, the French Canadians did too. It would have been more sensible to relate this movement to other nationalist movements in the world. It would soon have become clear that most campaigns for collective emancipation still have a nationalistic character, even today. And campaigns for colonial liberation obviously head the list. (This is another point that the Canadian movement and movements for decolonization have in common.) But it is unfortunately true that people did not understand any better than in the case of the Canadians that colonial liberation movements are national first and foremost, and only secondarily economic and social, at least from the chronological and strategic point of view.

Students: Do you believe that the best solution for these peoples lies in nationalism, and that there is any future in it?

Albert Memmi: There you are asking two different questions. I do not know whether the nationalist solution is a good one in the absolute.[1] It is difficult anyway to give any meaning to the phrase "in the absolute" when talking about politics. These countries are perhaps immature in comparison with Europe, which is in the process of outgrowing nationalism. It is still a fact that they have never known independence as nations, or at least not for a long time, and are crying out for it urgently. What seems to me important is that they have discovered that a nation wishing to free itself must first *re-assume its own responsibilities*. And this reassumption of responsibility still goes by the name of nationalism today.

The second question concerns the future of nationalist solutions. It is clear that the world is moving towards unification. Whatever the political obstacles, in a few years cultural unification, or at least unification as far as information goes, will have been achieved through the medium of television. It is only a question of transmission. And that is marvelous.

But it is not certain whether this integration on a worldwide scale will take place in any abstract sense, nor, above all,

[1] After reading my latest book, the French author Morvan Lebesque wrote to me suggesting that we fight for a "society of culture groups" rather than a society of nations. I do not reject this idea, but to be more precise I would say that I am as far as one can possibly be from adopting the Barresian ideal. In my opinion the nation is a means to an end, rather than the end itself: if nationalism is in a number of cases still the shortest road to emancipation for certain peoples, then the fight for national independence is the right one. If it is still necessary today to emphasize the cultural distinction of any one human group, in order to provide a legitimate reason for their emancipation, then we do have to stress the differences. It is so for the colonies, for the Jews, and so on . . . But it must be clearly understood that nations, culture, group differences must all be considered as part and parcel of the drive towards freedom.

THE COLONIZED

whether the question of authority will be involved. In other words, we have no right to demand that people suppress all the differences to which they cling, whether rightly or wrongly; or to use universal integration as an excuse for the domination of one community by another, of a minority by a majority group, or of one people by another.

Nationalism is in fact no more than the combination of the two claims implicit in the above. I am certain that if people were left in peace in these two respects, their national consciousness would be considerably dulled. What will survive remains to be seen, and no one can forecast that in advance. I personally feel it is of utmost importance that the domination which weighs so heavily on many groups of people as to distort their nature should cease. Worldwide integration would be furthered by its disappearance, I am sure.

Students: But, on a practical level, how can the "liberation" of the French Canadians be achieved?

Albert Memmi: I do not know. Perhaps it is not entirely for us to provide the answer, but for the Canadians themselves. We have returned here to the idea of *specific* domination that I spoke of at the beginning of our interview. Certain mechanisms are common to all kinds of domination; but in addition, each has its own individual character. This, incidentally, explains why so often even well-intentioned people do not *recognize* the existence of a situation where there is domination of one group by another. That is to say, they cannot see the similarity between it and other situations they know of. It is not difficult to point out immediately several differences between the plight of the French Canadians, and that of the Algerians under colonial rule, or of the Vietnamese today. And there are certainly many others. It is up to the Canadians to make a more exhaustive and detailed analysis of this. That was the substance of my reply to them last year: now that they have clearly stated that they are living under domination they must make plain what the peculiar nature of this domination is; because the kind of solution to be adopted will depend on the specific character of the problem. Any one solution does not necessarily hold good for every situation.

Students: There is not only the English colonization to consider. There are the Americans, too, on the doorstep, and even in the country itself. The Americans have such a hold over the Canadians that it is questionable whether they will ever manage to shake them off. Some say that a free Quebec will only be more open to Americanization.

Albert Memmi: Every fight for freedom seems at the outset slightly crazy. Those who are dominated are faced with an adversary very overpowering, who has in fact overpowered them and held them in slavery for so long, depriving them thereby of all collective means and strength to retaliate. And yet, look at Cuba, look at Vietnam! It seems at first incredible that such small nations can hold out for so long, and perhaps even be victorious, against such gigantic force.

That apart, the problem of Canadian resistance to America (if they really want to resist, of course) is today part of a generalized problem, a fact which at once makes it infinitely less desperate; or as difficult as for other nations. The whole world is struggling against American ascendancy, without quite knowing how to set about it. We are aware of it even here in France, and we have discovered too that American exploitation is infinitely more far-reaching than was thought. I admit that it may seem far more difficult to resist for Canada, alone in the midst of an English-speaking continent. In a way Canada is already virtually a colony of the United States, only that if the English Canadians submit with fairly good grace, the French Canadians refuse to do so. But the real question is still: will the whole world eventually be dominated by America, or is there to be a reshuffle, a new distribution of power? In the latter case, why should there not be a place for the Canadians in a world organized on this new basis?

Students: There is one last cause adopted by some of the

THE COLONIZED

French Canadians: an attempt to counter Christian education. Their argument is that Christian education has laid too much emphasis on belles-lettres and philosophy, and has left the real control of business affairs to the English, as a result of their Protestantism and their pragmatism.

Albert Memmi: There is no doubt that any community seeking independence must also *wage war on itself.* I discovered this inner conflict among the colonized, among the Jews and among the blacks. The North African writers denounced colonization: but nearly all of them also denounced the structure of their own institutions, their families and their scale of values. This fact was masked by the importance of the external conflict. And, of course, we must remember too, that these native traditions and values were for a long time of positive use in helping the dominated group to hold its own against its oppressors. That is why I suggested calling them *protective values.* For the French Canadians it was the Catholic religion that served as a refuge from the Protestant English. But after a time, protective values become limitating and have to be discarded.

Students: One last question: do you feel that the French Canadians are ready for a struggle such as you describe, to be fought on so many fronts? Do you not think that the hankering for comfort—American style—that is so strong in them, will keep them from joining the extremists?

Albert Memmi: There again, I have no idea. When it comes to making forecasts of that kind, I am not sufficiently familiar with the real state of affairs in Canada. There are only a few observations I can make. It is not necessary, as you well know, for there to be a large number of militant extremists. It is more important that they voice what the majority of the population feels, if only obscurely; when they do that, they almost always make themselves heard in the end. Now de Gaulle's visit made many people realize that a very large majority of French Canadians are responsive to ideas ranging from a wide measure of

Are the French Canadians Colonized?

self-government to complete independence. It was by no means just something staged by the press, as people have tried to insinuate.

The R.I.N., which used to be a quaint, story-book feature of Canadian life, is constantly gaining ground. How far will the Canadians go? That is the question. When I went there I was convinced of one thing: that there are far more young people than one would think who are ready to go to any lengths, and even to become martyrs to the cause. Let us hope that it will not be necessary.

(Translated By Jane Brooks)

7

*Franz Fanon
and the Notion of
"Deficiency"*

Recently, at an international symposium on sociology,[1] one of
the delegates thought he could challenge my description of the
colonized man by placing it against that given by Franz Fanon
and claiming that I had borrowed some of Fanon's ideas.

Although this kind of challenge is in bad taste, and despite
the fraternal respect I felt for Fanon, I would like to answer
both those points very briefly.

The second one is a matter of simple chronology. With the exception of *Peau noire, masques blancs* (*Black Skin, White
Masks*), all of Fanon's books were published after my own
Portrait du Colonisé (*The Colonizer and the Colonized*) in
1957. His *L'an V de la révolution algérienne* (*Year V of the
Algerian Revolution*) appeared in 1959, and *Les Damnés de la
Terre* (*The Wretched of the Earth*) in 1961. Meanwhile I was
writing my *Portrait of a Jew,* which was published in 1962; it
comes back to and explains many themes in *The Colonizer and
the Colonized.*

[1] VIth Symposium of the International Association of French-speaking
sociologists, at Royaumont, in October, 1965.

Franz Fanon and the Notion of "Deficiency"

Of course some comparison could be made between *The Colonizer and the Colonized* and *Black Skin, White Masks,* but that would easily reveal that Fanon's book was not yet the work of a sociologist but rather, of a phenomenalist and psychiatrist. Both the economic and the institutional aspects, which are important in my work, are almost totally missing from Fanon's book. They do not show up in his work until later.

So the least we can say is that any suggestion that I took ideas from Fanon cannot be taken seriously.[1]

It's not that I'm afraid to admit my sources. For instance, I am quite ready to acknowledge that I did not discover the importance of the economic aspect of colonization all by myself. Of course I lived it, first of all, like any other colonized person. But it was Marx and the Marxists who taught me how to conceptualize it. Marx's genius lies in having discovered the existence and the crucial role of the economic phenomena in all human situations. It was to be expected that they would crop up in the colonial relationship as well. I have tried, however, to make clear the special role and significance of what I have called the colonial *privilege.*

I have also demonstrated that the notion of privilege was not a purely economic one but was psychological and cultural too. My own effort has consisted of taking this foundation, or this critical dimension which is the economic relationship, and trying on that basis to describe the socio-cultural phenomena *peculiar* to colonization. Some are apparent in the colonizer, others in the colonized. This yields two complete portraits, each governed by the other and arranged by the objective colonial condition.

In this chapter I am not concerned with the colonizer, and I

[1] If we really wanted to take this parallel further, we would have to do more than compare *The Colonizer and the Colonized* alone to the whole of Fanon's work; we would have to extend the comparison to the two volumes of *Portrait of a Jew,* which takes a more general look at the mechanisms by which any oppression operates.

THE COLONIZED

would refer the reader to my book on the subject. As for the colonized, I have, it is true, emphasized the psychological and cultural destruction which take place in him.

Let me recall briefly that, in my opinion, there is a *mythical portrait* of the colonized; it is the colonizer who has drawn it, and it is mostly negative. But I have added that neither this mythical portrait nor its negativeness was entirely overdone, since:

a) they correspond to a certain number of real and concrete *deficiencies* in the colonized. For instance, the colonizer accuses the colonized of being lazy and of not working very hard. Slander pure and simple? Yes and no. It is slander to say that the colonized, as such, does not like to work. But it is true that the colonized is in fact *idle*. (Of course, this must be blamed on the structure of colonialism and not on the colonized himself.) Yet in a certain way there is real negativism in the relationship between the colonized and work. Only the interpretation differs, and it is the interpretation that changes everything.

b) The colonized *admits* that there is some truth in the accusations made by the colonizer. Whereas, according to my symposium challenger, Fanon said, "The colonized does not admit that this mythical portrait resembles him at all."

I maintain, on the contrary, that in every dominated man, there is a certain degree of *self-rejection*, born mostly of his downcast condition and exclusion. I have shown this, at some length, where the Jew is concerned too. How could we possibly expect anything different? When the objective conditions are so weighty and corrosive, how could we imagine that they will not result in some destruction, that they will not warp the soul, the behavior and even the physiognomy of the oppressed man? We cannot wiggle out of it by saying that "the colonized is made inferior but he is not reduced to servitude." I must apologize to Fanon: I do not by any means wish to belittle his courage and his unshakeable belief in a cause for which he gave his life, but

Franz Fanon and the Notion of "Deficiency"

saying that is dodging the issue. All we have to do is read the works of the black or North African writers, to find dozens of examples of fictionalized descriptions, based on experience, of the path I have tried to trace in my books, the one that leads inexorably from accusation to the reduction-to-nothingness, by way of depersonalization—cultural, scholastic, social and historical depersonalization.

I am told that in such and such a remote area of Tunisia or Algeria, in such and such a village, there is none of this self-doubt apparent, none of the humiliation felt by the colonized, nothing to bear out this portrait of the colonized. I am told, in other words, that the man in the portrait exists only in the cities and towns and especially among the intellectuals and the cultured classes.

But this actually confirms (and I am grateful at least for that) that for all colonized who are aware of their colonized condition, my portrait is a true likeness. I claim, though, that far more of the colonized are aware than is generally supposed, and that this awareness is not restricted only to the intellectuals.

But more important, isn't it clear that this so-called objection is actually a counter-proof? For doesn't it amount to saying that when there is no colonizer in the picture, when the *colonial relationship* is non-existent, the features characterizing the colonized fade away? I might also add that this objection, if it applies at all, could apply only to psychological, subjective features. Even if the colonized were in no way aware of his condition, that condition would exist no less *objectively*, and in all events he undergoes the effects of it. The various types of *deficiency* are not only subjective; they are also objective, economic, social, cultural. The entire life of the colonized is dependent, *even if he does not notice it.*[1]

---

[1] What separates me from Sartre is the importance which the *objective conditions* of oppression have for me. I have shown this with respect to the colonized man, as well as to the Jew or the black American.

For that matter, is Fanon's own thinking on this point really coherent? I too could cite a great many contradictory passages of his, where he speaks of "mutilation," "inferiorization," "criminal impulsion"—results, obviously, of colonization.

Actually I believe that, unlike my challenger, Fanon fully admitted that the personality of the colonized was affected in these ways. It is not possible that he did not observe them, either before or after I did. But he found them embarrassing and repulsive. This is because, like many other defenders of the colonized, he harbored a certain amount of revolutionary romanticism. The colonizer was the complete bastard, and the colonized the completely good man. As for most social romantics, so for him the victim remained proud and intact throughout oppression; he suffered but did not let himself be broken. And the day oppression ceases, the new man is supposed to appear before our eyes immediately. Now, I do not like to say so, but I must, since decolonization has demonstrated it: this is not the way it happens. The colonized lives on for a long time in the decolonized man, and we will have to wait longer still before we see that really new man. I can understand that this notion of *deficiency* is an unpleasant one. I had the same feeling when I described the deficiencies of the Jew.

Another important strain in Fanon's thinking is his accusation of the bourgeoisie in each nation. He tried to show its failure and its betrayal. But here again, we cannot tell whether he was announcing, *forecasting* their failure or whether he was hoping it would happen. Again, like the revolutionary romantics, Fanon has a lyrical way of sliding over realities: because they want certain things, they end up believing that these things must inevitably happen or have already happened. Whereas, whether we like it or not, in almost every country the bourgeoisie has come to power. For the time being, most colonies, in gaining independence, have given precedence to form

---

Not only is the oppressed man *considered* as such but also, and especially, he is *treated* as such.

(national) over content (social). And that is what I took the liberty of predicting, based on my analysis of most colonial relationships: it was probable that the domination of one people by another would resolve itself, first of all, into national liberations.

(*Translated by Eleanor Levieux*)

III

THE
JEW

(The preface to the French edition of
Freud and the Jewish Mystical Tradition by David Bakan,
D. Van Nostrand Co., Inc., Princeton, New Jersey.)

8

The Double Lesson of Freud

There is a paradox in Kafka. In the whole of the work published during his lifetime Kafka never once wrote the word "Jewish." However, his diary, published posthumously, reveals that he was literally haunted by his Jewishness, and that the whole of his work was an attempt to interpret, to put in order, to exercise his condition as a Jew. Freud was not so secretive about this aspect of himself: he dedicates an entire book to it, though admittedly at the end of his life; he presents a collection of the good old Jewish stories and reflects on the mechanics of Jewish humor; he never hesitates to declare himself Jewish. Although Freud's Jewishness is more obvious than Kafka's, it is perhaps not so necessary for the understanding of psychoanalysis. The work of Freud must be one of the most universal, both in its significance and in its repercussions, that history has ever known. It would be ridiculous to attempt to reduce it to individual or even national particularities. And Freud himself, although he does not conceal that he is a Jew, often worries about protecting his new science from a closeness with the personality of its creator that is too intimate and too dangerous for its diffusion. If one were obliged to give his work a genesis, one could say that it is European, Occidental, and—why not say the word—*Christian,* like the work of so many great modern Jews.

I will now make a confession: one does not write a preface for the sole purpose of presenting a book, or at least that is only the apparent but secondary aim of doing so. You defend another person's work because it also confirms your own ideas, and because the author is supporting you as much as you are him. After many assumptions and inquiries, I have been convinced for a long time that there would be a new and fairly complete study of Freud in the perspective of his Jewishness. I thought I had discovered that Jewishness was on the whole much more apparent than one believed in the behavior and thoughts, if not in the confessions of most Jews. In any case, it is so important to self-observant men such as artists and philosophers, that they cannot avoid showing evidence of it in their work, whether intentionally or not.[1]

And if this was valid in the cases of Kafka, Heine and Spinoza, why should it not be so of Freud, who returns so often to the subject of his Jewishness? Freud only wrote one book exclusively devoted to Judaism; however, references are by no means lacking throughout the whole of his completed works, and these amply suggest, or so it would appear, a sustained preoccupation with the matter. It was obvious that one day someone would collect and compare all these scattered references; there is no doubt that one would discover a considerable consistency in them.

David Bakan's work is more than satisfactory in this matter.

[1] I am convinced that someone should undertake a series of "Researches into Jewishness." As far as Kafka is concerned, this wish is being fulfilled in a remarkable way by Mme Ferenczi, who is preparing a thesis on the subject. Another member of my audience at the Ecole Prâtique des Hautes Etudes, Dr. Rousseau, has in fact devoted his thesis to Freud. Who will offer us, in this same perspective, a study of Proust, or even of Marx?

The Double Lesson of Freud

So much so, that I am not sure if I myself can reach the conclusion that he wants us to make: namely that Freudianism is a laic transformation of the Jewish mystique. Bakan would not take offense, since he gives us a sincere warning of the impossibility of providing us with definite proof. On the other hand, he has already clearly shown us something that I think is at least as important: the decisive importance of Freud's Jewishness in the formulation of his work, and therefore the need to be fully aware of this for the best interpretation of his work.

We have perhaps not taken enough notice of the impact on the whole of Jewish destiny felt during that terrible period which started around 1881, and which was the proclamation and the beginning of the complete extermination of central and eastern European Jewry. It ended, let us hope, with the Final Solution undertaken by the Nazis. (It recorded not only the death sentence of the Jewish community in these countries, but also the birth of the Jewry of America, where henceforth the majority of European Jews emigrated. In short, the physiognomy of modern Jewry dates from this period.) In any case, for more than twenty years Europe was to echo with the cries of the victims of atrocious pogroms, who were being punished for alleged ritual murders perpetrated by the Jews. Every now and then, a body was discovered, preferably that of a young woman who had been raped, drained of its blood by a Jew wishing to celebrate the Passover in the best way possible. The last charge, followed by a real trial, with real judges, lawyers, witnesses, and reports in the press, took place in Bohemia in 1899! Freud, who was twenty-five in 1881, therefore lived a great part of his adult life in this daily atmosphere of nightmare. Just imagine *France-Soir* with the following headline across the front page, "Three days to Passover, another child's corpse found in the rue des Rosiers." Kafka's entire work, the last manuscript of which is called *Amerika* surprisingly enough, is probably indebted to this pre-apocalypse. How could Freud not be deeply affected by it? We must already be grateful to David Bakan for providing us at this point with several sociological landmarks. These are generally very rare, one must admit, in the works of psychoanalysts.

Of course, the external conditions that surround the conception of a work are never enough to account for its internal structure, and in particular, for the details. Is it also necessary for these conditions to have echoed intimately in the personal history of the author? In which case, how did Freud live out his Jewishness? It was indeed at first a source of constant worry, it hampered his career, and even his own personal development, since he may well have decided to change direction when he realized that a Jew could not succeed in the field of pure research. Later when he was famous and universally admired, it was in spite of his Jewishness, which hindered the diffusion of his discoveries, and his complete recognition by others. However, this is how he experienced it, and he said so tirelessly, to his friend Fliess, to his wife, to his friends, most of whom were Jewish, to his students, who were rarely non-Jewish. In short, he suffered from anti-Semitism both objectively and subjectively. He lived out his Jewishness with discomfort and with hostility from others, at first as a heavy negativity.

But it is still not enough. He could have tried to put aside his Jewishness, as so many contemporary Jews forced themselves to do, often with apparent success. Freud could have evaded the problem that faces every Jew because of this. But this is precisely what he does not do. On the contrary, he frequently considers it, he increases the questions, he outlines partial answers, he returns to it constantly, right up until *Moses,* and until "I am an old Jew," which he said at the pinnacle of his glory, but in exile. If one assembled all the pieces, what would be the definitive and complete meaning of all these different endeavors? It seems obvious that Freud, in the manner of most contemporary great Jews (starting with Spinoza), devotes himself to a methodical questioning of his Jewishness in its double aspect: a denunciatory analysis of the aggression of others, and a reasoned revolt against the traditions of his own people.

For a very long time different generations of Jews have exerted themselves desperately to find explanations for anti-Semitism. The various explanations that Freud puts forward are not the least suggestive of them. His obviously provide both a confirmation and an extension of analytical theory: the root of hatred for the Jews lies in the unconscious of the people. There is an unconscious jealousy towards a race that considers itself chosen, and that oddly is treated as such. The poorly Christianized people are angry with the Jews for this contaminated gift: Christianity, the fear caused by the strange rites of circumcision, etc. . . . May I also suggest that the kind of hesitant but fundamental pessimism of Freudian thought could well originate from the feeling of insuperable Jewish misfortune? [1] Or in this obscure yet implacable hostility of the non-Jews?

Perhaps Bakan does not insist enough on this objective and exterior aspect of Jewish misfortune. The hostility of others is the negative side of the Jewish condition, and yet, alas, it is just as much a part of the modern Jew as is his positive Jewishness. But this was not Bakan's purpose and finally he is right, for nor was it Freud's main purpose. Although he came to be concerned with collective phenomena, Freud was neither an historian nor a sociologist. As for the hostility of others, he could only experience it, bemoan it, explain it a little, and above all, avoid it as much as possible. On the other hand, if, almost disarmed, he does ascertain that the non-Jews impose an unbearable oppression on the Jew that limits him in his professional,

[1] Perhaps just as much in the dedicated search for a common denominator among all men. One could say that the majority of great Jews have searched for some common factor that is above all differences, and joins together all of humanity, including the Jews; thus, Freud and instinctual universality; Marx and economy, the prime mover of history, Spinoza and God. . . .

social and historic life, Freud discovers that his own tradition is the cause of an even more disastrous oppression: one that binds from within. Sickness is his business, and he has a very thorough knowledge of the sick. The liberation of the Jew must include a very definite untying of intimate bonds, it must create a separation from his beliefs and collective practices, in short, it must suppose a preliminary rejection of his Jewishness. In any case, the result is that Freud is the modern Jew who delivered the greatest blow against Judaism. More radically than Marx, who accused it very artificially from the outside (Judaism: a philosophy of money). More than Spinoza, who, in spite of everything, remains on the level of concept and history. For Freud devotes himself to an interior analysis of direct Jewish experience.

It is here that the continuous reading of Freud's completed works in this perspective becomes particularly illuminating and reveals a coherent attitude. The Freudian contestation is obviously a settling of accounts, first with the Jewish religion, but certainly with the Christian religion as well, and finally with all religion. This is why the arguments that Freud puts forward aim at and eventually reach universality. However, he starts the discussion, more or less discreetly but without any hesitation, by looking at the religion of his family and childhood, the religion that he knew from within and whose tyrannical and obsessive nature he experienced himself. When Freud analyzes and denounces over-restrictive alimentary rituals and compares them to the rituals of the obsessed, must he not have been thinking of kosher restrictions? I have shown the enormous importance of the family in the life of every Jew, who is warmed by it, armed against the hostility of the world by it, yet at the same time over-protected and occasionally suffocated by it. Is it just a coincidence that the family environment is at the center of Freud's observations? And that he finds there both the source of neuroses and the condition of complete security for

The Double Lesson of Freud

the child and even for the adult? Have we not seen enough suffering from the Oedipus complex due to the awe-inspiring father of the Jewish family? One only has to look at the role of the father in Kafka's work. When one has lived in the atmosphere of a traditional Jewish family (such as Freud's father's family, and Freud's own family, for when it was his turn, he too played the part of patriarch!) how easy it is to understand this insistent advice to rid oneself of the father! Bakan is entirely right in suggesting that the matter can be traced back to *Totem and Taboo*.

Moses is by no means a unique or unusual meditation. On the contrary, it is completely in perspective with this questioning of the whole of Jewish tradition: it is the most systematic attempt, the most direct and finally the most complete answer to a constant preoccupation. And let me say at once that I find this book fascinating. I am amused by the embarrassment of analysts when they are faced with this so-called failure of the Master, and by the jubilation of traditionalists caused by a demonstration based on so many historical errors. For I find this book infinitely more valuable, more suggestive, and, in spite of everything, more real than anything that the historians have attempted to discover about Moses, which is not very much, and which will never have great importance. For it is not just a matter of history. And all those who, with the ashamed and resigned consent of his disciples, tried to pick a quarrel with Freud, had hardly any effect on him. Freud did make mistakes, of course, although all he did was to pick up certain errors made by authentic historians (he chose the parts that suited him from the specialists, but which of us does not do the same?). It is quite likely that Moses was not Egyptian, that there never were two Moseses, that the Hebrews may not have killed him, etc. . . . But Freud, with great shrewdness, understood something that the historians did not: that Moses is, above all, a myth, by which I mean that his physiognomy and his behavior as they are imagined are far more important than his actual physiognomy and behavior. For this fictitious character was created by a whole people who express themselves through him. Brigitte Bardot as the French imagine her and dream about her goes far beyond the real Brigitte Bardot as the historians see her, who is nothing more than a mediocre little bourgeoise, neither very intelligent, nor very beautiful. Of course the historian must do his work, if only to give a concrete though often derisory base to the myth. But then it is necessary to describe the importance of the myth, to explain how much of themselves the French have put into the myth of Bardot. So Freud did not even need this great historical construction in order to establish his Moses. That side of it was not his job and, furthermore, he had made mistakes. Let us not be guilty of Freudolatry. It is quite pointless to suspect Freud of any Machiavellianism or even quite simply of any esoterism in this book. There is no proof of it here, or indeed anywhere else. There is so little allegory in *Moses* that the book is almost the opposite. It sets out to destroy an allegory: the way that the Jews represent Moses, or in other words, their law and themselves. By leaning on historical facts Freud wants to demonstrate that this person did not exist. His only mistake was to lean on historians who were at fault. Let us apply his own method to him and ask ourselves why he chose to lean on those historians, and to give preference to those alleged facts.

Obviously, it was because it helped his demonstration and his struggle, which however were quite sufficient in themselves and in no need of assistance from history. Moses is significant of Judaism, to such an extent that Mosaism and Judaism are considered equivalents. Moses personifies Jewish tradition and law, everything that binds the Jew from within.

With the desire to liberate the Jew from this interior oppression, Freud methodically attacks the Jew's most prestigious and tenacious collective dream, the myth of Moses. For myths are the waking dreams of humanity, and Moses is the collective myth of the Jews. We are dealing with a psychoanalytical procedure, admittedly applied to a whole group of people, but there is an extension in its meaning: to become a man one must kill one's father. To liberate the Jews one must kill Moses. But not by means of an historical demonstration. It is true that history is called to the rescue and used with too much ingenuity perhaps, but over and above the character and the history of Moses, the whole of Judaism itself is implicated. That is also why Freud hesitates before publishing his texts (as any Jew would hesitate before speaking in public about his traditions and his people). One does not attack the unconscious, either individual or collective, without great care. The guardians of tradition were not mistaken in hating Freud (although they did not admit it openly because Freud is too important) and in preferring Jung, oddly enough, his non-Jewish and slightly anti-Semitic disciple: *Freud wants to liberate the modern Jew from Judaism.*

We now seem to have reached a new paradox, Freud's this time. Kafka, who was so obsessed with his Jewishness that he dedicated his whole work to it, systematically wipes out all traces of it. Freud, who decided to face it head-on, devotes himself to a merciless dismantling of Judaism. In fact, although it is expressed by two different temperaments, we are dealing with the same fundamental attitude: an examination in revolt of an unacceptable condition. In both cases the result is the same: the denial of Judaism.

It is at this point that Bakan comes in again: this denial, far from being an exceptional scandal in the history of Judaism, is an interior phenomenon that recurs periodically and that is perhaps just as important as the respectful consent that remains in the path of tradition. I must say that I absolutely agree with him on this matter: a revolt against Judaism could well be an interior revolt against Jewry. It is yet another way of seeing oneself as Jewish. I also maintain that there is no reason for comparing Freud's ideas with those of the mystic Jews, just as there was no reason for finding an allegory in his work. Nor was Freud disguising a Jewish message in an attempt to reach the non-Jewish world.

David Bakan's attempts are once again fascinating and most suggestive: basically he is trying to give some distinction to this denial. Thus, this re-evaluation of tradition would quite simply be part of another tradition, of another heritage that is authentically Jewish, since it passed by way of the Cabal and led to Hassidism. I am also convinced that the wish to renew Judaism is one of the meanings of Jewish mysticism. It is true that this has often been perverted, as with Sabbatai Zvi's conversion to Islamism or with Frank's to Christianity. But these failures were quite probably revolts that turned sour because they could not yet be accomplished historically. They were, however, most essential: one had to begin by confronting the rabbinical order, by shaking the institutions of the community, and by daring to criticize openly the letter of the law. Furthermore, when one was faced with an ideology that had been closed in on itself for centuries, and that had defended itself at every step by whatever means possible, be they betrayal or banishment, any pursuit, any novelty, however timid, immediately appeared to be provocative and dangerous. The only hope for rebellion is for it to succeed. It is then integrated, even unwillingly, and is henceforth part of the heritage. Thus it is that Hassidism, once so strongly attacked, is now one of the solutions to the crisis of modern Judaism; the same can be said of the Haskala. Such is the necessary drama of all Jewish modernity: a preliminary struggle that negates tradition.

It is just as fascinating to follow Bakan's literally dizzy comparisons, which are all the more worrying because they rely on technical data, between the Cabal and psychoanalysis. When one has been reminded of the importance of the dream and its interpretation in Jewish mystic tradition it is quite legitimate to ask oneself whether Freud did not search there for the pivot of his doctrine: the dream, key to the unconscious. Similarly,

The Double Lesson of Freud

when one considers the extraordinary use of erotic symbolism in the Cabal, one is less taken aback by the surprising importance attached to sex by Freudianism. The methods of concentration and inward reflection, used for so long by the Cabalists, do not seem strange to analysts. One can well understand how tempting it is to reach the conclusion that there is a direct relationship, and that this conclusion clinches the argument. It is almost too simple. Freud decided to come to grips with his Jewishness; he is led to refuse traditional Judaism; in so doing, he has the authority of a long heretical tradition: the mystic tradition. Conclusion: psychoanalysis finds its exact genesis in this same Jewish mysticism.

Perhaps. Freud never mentioned it, however. We have no *proof* that Freud ever read or even knew the writings of the mystics. Is it perhaps a deliberate camouflage? Freud could have carefully hidden this source because he feared that it would harm his doctrine. In this case we can interpret his work historically, as in the case of *Moses*. There is nothing to prove it. Freud was not an artist, but a thinker. For Kafka, the use of symbols and allegory was the very stuff of his work. Freud specialized in truth. It is certain that many men who dealt with truth were forced to disguise their discoveries. But Freud almost always ended by telling all. He hesitated before publishing *Moses* but finally he did publish it. If, once or twice, he did not put his name to some text, it was mainly because he was not sure that the psychoanalytical method was applicable to the subject matter. The same can be said of the meditation in front of Michelangelo's Moses. It is a form of modesty, and also a way of not devaluating the label, just as a playwright prefers to sign a scientific work with a different name. But even so, Freud does not hesitate to draw from the good old Jewish stories for the composition of *Wit and Its Relation to the Unconscious*. Finally, there is his large correspondence with his wife and his friends: he never mentions this source. Why not believe him? Must one belittle the conscious and manifested will on the pretext that the unconscious and the hidden are of such great importance, especially when one is dealing with such a well-informed thinker as Freud?

On the other hand, just because of this one omission, how can we eliminate other essential sources? I will not hark back to Freud's Christian governess whose importance Freud himself stressed, nor more generally to the mediation of Christianity, which is so evident in the thoughts of so many contemporary Jews, who often only find Judaism by means of it. I want to discuss German Romanticism in particular: the German cultural connection is just as crucial as the Jewish connection in order to understand Freud. The quotations are many on this matter. Freud was a man of German culture, and a very cultured man at that. I think it is quite possible, for example, to make a systematic and parallel comparison between the preoccupation of the German Romantics with the dream and the various processes concerning the dream that are enumerated and classified by psychoanalysis. The French surrealists became aware of this relationship and laid claim to both of these elements. Indeed the whole matter may well spring from here. The German Romantics were probably aware of the Cabal, which had more influence on the German tradition than on the French, for example. One must surely conclude that Freud was directly inspired by the authors that he knew and admired, Freud, who gave so much credit to the spontaneous discoveries of writers. This brings us back to the problem of mediation. This source seems to be so important that I would more willingly propose a double genesis for Freudianism: Jewishness and German Romanticism.

For is it really necessary to trace his Jewish source back to mysticism alone? The dream is important in the whole of learned Jewish tradition, and in the Talmud as well, from which Bakan himself remembers the curious Berakoth treatise. Better still, the dream is part of the popular tradition. I speak from experience. The working-class quarters in Tunis were fas-

The Double Lesson of Freud

cinated by stories and interpretations of dreams, and by omens. And let us never forget that this daily living culture is also an aspect of Jewishness. So even if we are not certain that Freud read the Jewish mystics, it was not really necessary for him to have read them. In the same way, the astonishing role of sexuality in the Cabalistic structure has perhaps been extended to the libido, the centerpiece of psychoanalysis. It is by no means impossible. But then erotic life has always held a conscious and almost honored role in Jewish family life. I do not exclude an indirect and popular influence of the Cabal, which eventually succeeded in permeating all Jewish life. But instead of looking for a direct genesis of psychoanalysis in the Cabal, I would prefer to say that *the same social environment that produced mysticism could just as well have produced Freud.*

However, over and above this common ground, Freud's attitude is finally the exact opposite of the Cabalists'. I hope the author will forgive me: I often found that his interpretation was more Jungian than Freudian, and I admit that I am very wary of this particular aspect of Jung's interpretation of Freudianism. He seems to be saying that Freud has burned his fingers by prying into the unconscious and the irrational, and that he has involuntarily resurrected sorcery and the Devil! Although Freud did re-introduce the irrational, which had been strictly banned, into psychology, he did not resurrect it. *He rationalized the irrational,* which is not at all the same thing. Nor, as Jung often suggests, did he resurrect the sacred as such. He did, certainly, attempt to find a meaning for the sacred as such, and showed that it was not just pure fantasy. But by giving it a different meaning from the one that tradition gave it, by ridding it of fear and restriction, by reducing it to a personal interior drama with no reference to divinity, he secularized it. Far from seeing a sign of nostalgia for the divine in eroticism, Freudianism reduces this nostalgia to a more or less disguised erotic aspiration. In short, Freud never proposed a new concept of tradition and of the sacred that would save them as such. Nor did he even attempt to preserve Jewish law by means of a new interpretation. He tries to fit everything that he deals with into the realm of science. How can we forget that he is above all, and deliberately so, a scientist? Freud said himself of his theory of the dream that it was "a plot of new land won for science, against popular prejudices and against mystique."

One can maintain that laicization is perhaps the only way of saving Jewish tradition. Such an adaptation alone would permit the Jewish heritage to be taken up once again and henceforth continued by the Jew (and this is precisely what Freud is doing). But one must make no secret of it, and Bakan is well aware of this. The laicization of Jewish tradition is to be found first of all in its negation, in the way that it is understood and lived by its believers, and in the way that it proposes itself to them. This negation is much needed, because Judaism, which for so long helped the Jews to live, has become impossible to live with today. The Jew, who today wants to make advances in the field of knowledge and of liberty, who wants to live together with the others, must begin with this rebellion, or must at least show indifference to the law and its institutional manifestations. There is a certain ingratitude to be found here. Just as the father protected the child during its early youth, so the law protected the people during their threatened childhood. But just as the father must stand aside for the child to become a man, so the tyranny of Moses must be overcome for the modern Jew to be liberated.

We are not dealing with a new paradox. After this last war, many people repeated, following a well-known writer who was quoted as saying so, that one had to assert oneself, and that the oppressed in particular had the duty of asserting themselves. People understood this statement to mean that they had to claim no matter what belief, no matter what collective practice, even if it meant destroying its very reason. One must beware of

The Double Lesson of Freud

confusing "to assert oneself" with "to accept oneself." On the contrary, I believe that the oppressed can only assert themselves by first rejecting themselves, by dissipating the ideology of misery and the exorcisms that they created during their long dark night. Certainly this has allowed the Jew to survive, but in return it keeps him in a state of resigned helplessness. *Self-rejection is the first step on the path of revolt and liberation.* In any case, the denial of himself as a traditional Jew is the necessary price that the modern Jew must pay if he is to escape from oppression, both interior and exterior.

That is Freud's first lesson. But his second, which is perhaps just as important although Freud does not discuss it as much, is that this denial does not go right to the very end: *the contestation of Judaism does not mean the rejection of Jews.*[1] In fact, it means just the opposite, since Freud's aim is to save his own kind and to save himself as a Jew, and since this rebellion must liberate the Jew from all that oppresses him. One can, indeed one must, reject Judaism, but one cannot reject Jewry, of which one is part, at least because one is not part of the others. It is not for a lack of courage or only for solidarity. Freud showed enough audacity during his extraordinary journey into the depths of himself. Without talking of pride, it is an almost therapeutic necessity, a degree of mental hygiene. One cannot reject oneself completely without the risk of destroying oneself. When one is already part of a minority and banned by society, one cannot allow oneself to break with one's own people as well. Rejected by others and rejecting one's own kind, what would become of one? The ground would slip away under one's feet. There is no doubt that those who are a part of a minority can better withstand separation and desertion by feeling that they belong to their own group. This

[1] This is why it is important to make a clear distinction between "Judaism" and "Jewry." Judaism is the sum total of doctrines, beliefs and institutions. Jewry is the sum total of existing Jews. Freud discusses Judaism, he never questions the fact that he is part of Jewry.

THE JEW

is their only reliable trump-card: *Jewishness becomes a positive force once again.* This is the meaning of the important advice that Freud gave to Graf who asked him whether he should convert his son: no, because he would lose everything, and he would not even be able to defend himself anymore.

That is not all. After fighting the might of the law, after dismantling the fortress of tradition, after killing Moses, Freud can now allow himself to pick up the most useful pieces that are left, to be nourished by them and thereby strengthen himself for his difficult battle. It is a new feast at the expense of the totem. By executing Moses, he executes the law in its role of divine commandment, but he keeps the vital part, the commandment that he interprets as it suits him, that can glorify him. He repeats that he is proud to belong to the people that gave the Bible to the world. He remarks that oppression gave the Jew certain special qualities: the habit of solitude, of distance, of a critical mind. He suggests that only a Jew could have created psychoanalysis, etc. . . . In fact, he recovers his Jewishness, but this time as a cultural tradition and as a collective psyche.

So now we have Freud's answer in its entirety. To the question that history asks the modern Jew Freud replies: Jewishness is both negative and positive; the Jewish condition must be both rejected and accepted. Is it not obvious that most great modern Jews, each in their own way, have made the same reply? And that it is probably the only possible reply? Whether it be Herzl, the founder of the State of Israel, who had suddenly thought of a collective conversion, or Spinoza, whose position was clouded by the hatred of the devout, basically they both made the same proposal: one must cut off the old branch for new buds to blossom forth. At first it is only by rejecting Judaism that one can better assume one's Jewishness. There is no contradiction here, unless it be the very contradiction of Jewish existence. We must thank David Bakan for showing us that the mystics had already noticed this contradiction and that there

The Double Lesson of Freud

exists a genuine tradition of rejection. Freud described and experienced this very drama of the modern Jew: Freud or an exemplary Jewishness.

(*Translated by Carol Martin-Sperry*)

(Published in the Bulletin Saint Jean-Baptiste, June-July, 1966.)

9

Jews and Christians

It scarcely makes sense that I should be addressing you here: this is a meeting of believers, and of monotheists, and, as the chairman of this meeting has reminded you, I am a lay Jew.

But as everyone assures me I must speak, and in precisely this role, so that this point of view may be voiced and included in the general argument, I shall speak as a lay Jew.

I can, and even must, tell you quite plainly—as this is what you expect of me—that to my mind, *if the problem of the relations between Jews and Christians, and between Jews and Muslims, could be expressed only in theological terms, then it would be insoluble.*

For some time now people have been saying: "Let us return to the source; let us re-examine together the old texts; *they* have no anti-Semitic bias . . ." (I should hope not! They were written by Jews!). Certainly this should be done; it would be useful to everyone. But we still ought to take into account what Christianity has *become;* the *evolution* of Christians over the centuries.

Historically, the Jew occupies a negative place in the Christian drama: he is the counterpoint, the somber antithesis of the Christian. This is not my idea; it is taken from Christian writers. I could make innumerable, often unpleasant, citations from their works to support this theory. One thing is certain, and that is that Judaism and Jewry have for centuries been the Christians' stumbling-block, and this persistent, living reminder of their incomplete victory, and their continuing weakness, has exasperated them. The Jews have suffered horribly as a result of this exasperation.

In theological terms this is expressed in the drama of the crucifixion and the curse which was to fall on the Jews. Here too there is abundant written evidence.

"*Historically* the responsibility of the Jewish nation for the crucifixion may be attenuated; but, theologically, the fact remains that it was the Jews who put Jesus to death, and that it could not be otherwise." (Jean Pépin, professor and theologian.)

The result is a real and total *impasse*. An admirable man, and one whom I esteem highly, Jacques Madaule, the President of the Amitiés Judéo-chrétiennes, wrote not so long ago: "Thus the Jewish race are eternally blessed in the rod of Jesse, and eternally accursed in those of its sons who condemned Christ."

In 1963, some time after the opening of the Council, Father Daniélou, a founding member of the Amitiés Judéo-chrétiennes, reasserted his "conviction that the whole of Israel will one day acknowledge in Christ the fulfillment of its hope." (*Dialogues with Israel*, last page, ed. La Palatine.) He was merely repeating what he had stated even more clearly some years earlier: "The Jews and Muslims will be saved, not by Moses, nor by Mahomet, but by Jesus Christ alone . . . There is no possible compromise . . . There is an immovable antagonism that we have no right to minimize in our desire for a reconciliation." ("Judaism, Christianity, Islam.")

THE JEW

I must admit that I prefer frankness like this on both sides to any attempt to build on ill-defined foundations.[1]

Sadly, I must add one last citation, from the most recent Papal declaration: "They are grave and sorrowful pages where we read of the conflict between Jesus and the Jewish people, that people predestined to receive the Messiah, and nurtured in that expectation and that certitude alone, which, when Christ came, spoke and revealed himself, not only did not recognize him, but condemned, mocked and finally killed him."

These words were spoken on April 4th, 1965, in the Church of Notre-Dame de la Guadaluppe, while the Council was still in full session, and they have never officially been denied.

All this must be reconsidered, I suppose . . . But I may be forgiven, I hope, if I appear, to say the least, frightened by the magnitude of the task facing the Christian theologians.

More so since the same is true on the Jewish side. It is less widely known, because Christian opinion makes itself felt more readily, but on the theological plane, the Jewish refusal is just as categorical.

"The Jew is incomprehensible to the Christian: he is the die-hard who refuses to see what has actually taken place, and the Christian is equally incomprehensible to the Jew: for he has the presumption to claim that the redemption is a *fait accompli. There is no human force strong enough to bridge this gap.*"

These words were written by a man out of favor with Ortho-dox Jews, but whom I greatly admired. This was Martin Buber, in my opinion the greatest Jewish philosopher of modern times. Only a few weeks ago in *Le Monde,* a young Orthodox rabbi

[1] Daniel-Rops, the most widely read of Christian writers, even went so far as to say "it may be that, in the equity of divine dispensation, it does not behoove Christian charity to prevent the horrors of the pogrom from compensating the insupportable horror of the crucifixion." I have perhaps misunderstood, but is he not proposing to countenance mas-sacre?

who broadcasts on the French television, confirmed this statement of Martin Buber's.

And so I was amazed that all the Jewish speakers present could perform such a tour de force as to speak for half an hour on the religious differences between Jews and Christians, without ever once mentioning Christ. But even this omission is significant: it is perhaps impossible to bring about a reconciliation between Jews and Christians—I repeat, as far as theology is concerned—so long as the central figure of Christ remains what it is for Christians and what it is for Jews. Personally, I would rather give up the attempt than hope for a solution in that direction.

So, what can be done?

Christianity, like Judaism in fact, is fortunately not only a theology, but a philosophy and a system of ethics too; a way of life and a collection of rules of conduct; *I suggest we study the problem from the opposite angle.*

This is when it can be useful to have the opinion of a lay Jew (I too am at last coming round to the idea). Instead of taking theology or mysticism as our starting point (not that I underrate the mystical experience, needless to say. Everyone must try to get at the meaning of life in his own way, and that particular one is not mine. All things considered, I prefer the poet's way, but that is another story altogether), instead of beginning with an ideology, I suggest that we look first at *the objective condition of the lives of those concerned.* The Christians must agree to considering the reality of the Jewish condition, for—forgive me for this reminder—they have done their bit in making it what it is. For there is *an objective Jewish condition* imposing itself on all Jews, believers and non-believers alike. There is a Jewish community and a Jewish solidarity, that is both negative and positive, both under threat and in the affirmation of essential unity. I do not for a moment share the faith of the Jewish speakers here, but I know that my destiny is closely linked with theirs, and in all my actions I confirm my solidarity with them.

If I were asked what I hope for from Christians and from Jewish-Christian dialogues, I should say that I want them to help me *effectively* to avert the threat (and, of course, for them not to oppose me any more themselves); also for them really to accept me as I am, and finally to acknowledge our differences, which are not only theological, but social, historical and cultural; for them to recognize my right to *all* the different aspects of my nature.

To my way of thinking this is *the only true ecumenism,* the touchstone of the new spirit of good-will animating Christians today. I hope I may be forgiven this whimsical notion; I think the theologians will come round to it later.

The problem is the same with regard to the Muslems: theology teaches us that Ismael was driven into the desert with his mother Agar, their only means of subsistence a little gourd of water. From this iniquitous expulsion Islam was born: how could this mythical act ever be expiated?

On the other hand, we can, and we must, come together to study *present-day relations* between Jews and Muslems, and on the basis of them establish new rules of conduct.

I think, however, that the theologians already *are* coming round to this point of view, and are beginning to examine their conscience. A sign that the Church is already changing in a very real sense. The Catholic Church has finally condemned colonization; its economic and social concepts are undergoing revision; the priests in Spain have come down from their ivory towers! Who knows? Perhaps the Church will make a stand on the subject of Vietnam. Is there not one further tiny proof of all this in the fact that I, a lay Jewish writer, am here among you, and that you are listening to me with good-will?

(*Translated by Jane Brooks*)

IV

THE
PROLETARIAT

(Preface to *Une Société anonyme*,
by Christiane Peyre, Juilliard, 1962.)

10

Does the Worker Still Exist?

Apparently, there are no longer any workers. This is the latest
excuse that the middle classes have found. Look, they say, all
the members of the working classes now have scooters and tel-
evisions; they go to the movies frequently and take regular holi-
days; in a little while they will be helping to run the factories.
Yes, it is true that over the past few years stocks have been
going up and huge profits are to be had; but this doesn't hurt
anyone, since everybody takes advantage of it. Hard labor or
dangerous work? It is the foreigners who do those jobs; French
people don't like work any more. In any case, now we have
automation . . . in short, stop telling us about working-class
conditions: in our country they don't exist any more.

The only trouble is that it is always the middle classes talking; they are the ones who ask the questions and supply the
answers, ever since they came to power. Whereas the only
really valid reply to any query about the working classes should
come from the workers themselves. And they, up to now, have
always been silent. This is why Mme Peyre's book is so precious
to us, for she is a worker, writing of her life as a worker.

THE PROLETARIAT

Testimonies of this kind have always been very rare. There is scarcely any working-class literature. There are the writings of Georges Navel, and a few craftsmen's journals. But craftsmen, however destitute, are wholly independent persons; and Navel, admirable though he is, organized his life in just such a way as not really to fit into the category of worker. He preferred to live on figs, and bread when he could get it, to keep the wolf from the door. That is what gives his work its piquancy: he is a free man. The workers, on the other hand, have scarcely raised their voices throughout the whole course of history, for they do not know how to speak, they have not learned the art. And even if, by some miracle, they were to acquire this gift, ridiculous as it may seem, they would have neither the strength nor the time to use it. (Is not this silence, this inability, or this lack of opportunity, in itself a glaring proof that they are still oppressed?)

This seems to me the very heart of the matter in Mme Peyre's book. To the question: can one still speak of the plight of the working class, Mme Peyre, a worker and the daughter of a working-class man, who by chance has learned to speak out and so can save herself, replies: yes, there is certainly such a thing, and it is terrible. On this subject she has written what are probably the best pages of the book. They must be read to understand what it means, even now, in our day, to work in a factory. First there is the noise, "the huge vibration" of the machines; then the rhythm, so rapid that, even if it is regulated, "the least hitch is enough to make you panic"—you no longer know which way to turn; then "your hands counting the kilos," all sense of time lost, your head growing emptier and emptier until it reels. "There *is* no more time," insists the author, in one particularly compelling passage. In the end one is reduced to the level of an object, a machine of flesh and blood, accessory to the metallic monsters: "I have eyes only to watch my machines, feet only to run from one to another, hands only to feed them." It is not common knowledge, but workers often take drugs to help them fight this mechanized stupor. The worker's condition is a prison, a kind of hell.

I am very much afraid that this description will suit nobody, for even socialist countries, which by definition aim at the welfare of the working classes, are committed to industrialization. I am well aware that, for better or for worse, we have entered on what the experts call the technico-industrial era. But we must determine, without trying to cheat or to shift responsibility, what effect the technical-industrial era has on the life of the worker. This book is not a work of fiction, but a diary of day-to-day observations made during a whole year of a worker's life. It is better that it should be so. While we may scruple to believe a work of the imagination, we cannot challenge documentary evidence. And this document, on a Parisian refinery, is ruthless.

Obviously, in spite of what we have just said, working conditions have improved, in contrast to what they were a century ago. Canteens have been repainted, shower facilities have been increased, and sometimes lawns have been planted (although in the factory in question the cloakrooms are still filthy, and the factory girls eat their midday meal on upturned buckets). Of course the standard of living has risen considerably. But we are still very far from the goal. And I think we will always be just as far, because it is probably not *minor improvements* of this kind that really matter. I do not want to put into Mme Peyre's mouth things she did not intend to say, but it seems to me to stand out very plainly from what she tells us that the condition of the working classes is *fundamentally one of oppression,* and not just incidentally so, in one aspect or another. With the result that, though you can air-condition the prison, you cannot make it less of a prison . . . unless you renounce the whole principle of the thing.

This consideration makes the argument about total or relative impoverishment somewhat futile. It is clear that workers

THE PROLETARIAT

today earn more than before: obviously the richer the capitalism of any given country, the greater the workers' profit. It would be absurd to maintain anything to the contrary. (Though here again, the worker never benefits to the same degree as his employer from an increase in the national revenue.) But it is above all important to recognize that the pressure brought to bear on the worker is not only economic. It would be wrong to try and describe the condition of the worker in purely economic terms. It is certain that in a society where basically everything can directly or indirectly be bought or sold, it is a terrible tragedy to be poor. And it is true that poverty is still the most striking feature of working-class life, what distinguishes it fundamentally from the plight of women or of Jews. But it is also true that the oppression suffered by the working class is a *total* oppression, affecting *every* aspect of the worker's life, and even influencing his dress, his carriage and his behavior.

This is why an improvement in material conditions does not make much of a difference. (It is a very relative amelioration in any case. This manna from heaven fallen into the laps of the workers—we should not exaggerate the importance of this either. The statistics are still far more revealing than all the biased nonsense that is said about the disappearance of the working class. Incidentally, female workers are still far and away worse off than male.) [1] This is why a higher standard of

[1] It is not so long ago that automation was supposed to have done away with working-class drudgery; then it was the "industrial society"; now it is computers. This is just one more piece of stupidity, or humbug. Not that there has not been a remarkable improvement. But to improve is not enough; the workers' lot, basically a state of utter dependency, must be revolutionized.

If only people were willing once again to listen to the opinions of those chiefly concerned, that is the workers themselves. Here is the latest testimony to date, 1967:

"The world of work is . . . totally closed and set apart. When you are in it you feel like an outcast, cut off from society, to such a degree that in the end you are not even revolted by it. You are someone who

living is not enough to make any serious difference to the circumstances of the working class. The problem is infinitely more
complex than that: the victim of oppression has to be transformed into a free man. For the worker is not simply a poor
man, he is above all a *dependent* creature. Though I repeat, he
is too, and he remains, a pauper. The search for food, clothing,
and a place to live, is a desperate one, the author shows us this
too, but the most tragic thing is the lack of independence that
constantly singles the worker out from his fellows. His economic distress, however great, is only one aspect of it. Since it
is through his work that the worker comes into contact with his
employer, it is especially in his work that the stigma of his dependent status is most cruelly evident. The worker is subjected
to things, and to men; he is the slave of a rhythm that is not his
own, of a time that he cannot control; he is made use of by men
who despise him, for, however horrible it may sound, it is true
that workers are scorned by their employers. How otherwise
would the latter dare to treat them as they do? How otherwise
would they not be afraid of them, because the workers are so
many and so strong? It is a fact, though, that an employer is
often capable of treating his employee like an animal: read, for
example, the description of how new workers are taken on;
witness this account of a female worker undergoing her medi-
cal examination: "The doctor, sitting squarely in his armchair,
looked me up and down for a moment, then said: 'You aren't
pregnant, are you? Are you sure? That weight over there, pick
it up . . . good, you're tough, that will do. Bend down. Fur-

---

doesn't count, who only serves to produce. It is when you emerge
from this world that the revolt begins."

"I should like to repudiate this idea that is current everywhere
. . . that poverty no longer exists."

Claude Etcherelli, interview with
Simone de Beauvoir, *Nouvel Observateur*, November 15, 1967.
By way of a reminder, I will also cite A. Andrieux and J. Lignon's
excellent piece of research, *"L'ouvrier d'aujourd'hui,"* which led them to
draw the same conclusions. (Paris, 1960, ed. Riviere, preface by P. Na-
ville.)

ther, further, get on all fours. I want to see your teeth . . . you're really quite sure you're not pregnant?' . . ." Slaves to their work, and tortured by it, they are no longer considered as human beings. (I was going to say as individuals, but realized that I would make the employers laugh, and even the workers themselves perhaps.) Even their most elementary physiological needs are disregarded. In Mme Peyre's book there are one or two jokes reminiscent of the bitter humor of Chaplin: for instance, the one about the heroine who wants to blow her nose and can never manage it, because of the ceaseless pounding of the machine; or "taking one's turn to pee," when the worker has to wait for someone to take over from him before he is allowed to go and relieve himself. How pleasant if just for a few months these fine gentlemen and these high-minded sociologists, who wink and say "The proletariat? Finished! An outmoded notion!" were to be harnessed to an assembly chain. It is still true to say that the world in which the worker spends the greater part of his existence is simply not made for him; this work, which eats away the best of his life, also eludes him completely. He is a cog in the machine, and not even an indispensable one at that, since workers are to be found in plenty and can always be replaced. So it is inevitable that they should be treated like beasts, or like objects, and valued less than the working stock itself, for that at least cost a lot in the first place. From the workers' point of view, it is no less inevitable that their work should not interest them. How can they possibly be interested in it? There are a few fleeting references in this book to the pleasure to be had from handling raw materials. Then boredom takes over, waiting for the next exhausting shift. "I discover monotony . . . the insipid flavor of monotony." The presence of an all-pervading *ennui* in the working class has already been pointed out, an occasion of surprise to many. But how could things be otherwise?

Mme Peyre makes no secret even of certain unpleasant traits among the workers, and this is something to be appreciated, for

it is never easy to remind those to whom one belongs of their
faults. In addition, one gives others a chance to preen themselves on their superiority, which is both disturbing and irritating. She admits, for instance, the kind of grudging respect that
her heroine feels for her employers, those well-fed, well-dressed
men, just because they lead an easy life and dress stylishly.
Yes, the oppressed admires his oppressor! She admits, too, the
curious obscenity of these women, an obscenity not confined to
their language . . . But at the same time she does try to explain these failings. In the author's opinion, obscenity, for these
downtrodden women, is only a way of expressing tenderness,
of establishing communication, of breaking through the solitude of each one in this infernal din. The love that the author
feels for those to whom she belongs is perhaps the most touch-
ing thing in this book.

We must also make it quite clear that she did not intend this
book to be a cry of despair. She is not particularly pessimistic,
and she makes as much as she can of the potential good qualities of her companions in affliction: a ray of sunlight or a
friendly word is enough to cheer them up; a few days' holiday,
and life is once more "simple and good." She fights for her
cause in the trade unions because she has had a glimpse of
possible ways to alleviate the workers' distress. She does not
even despair of the employers. She is a Christian and, as such,
unconcerned with the class struggle. She believes first and foremost in the power of persuasion to obtain the much-needed
improvements from the employers: "The bosses—they're Christian, aren't they, for goodness' sake? They ought to be able to
understand if we explain to them. They've got their heads in
the clouds, they don't realize, and it's not entirely their fault."
She succeeds in getting an appointment with the board of di-
rectors, to be exact chiefly by virtue of her earlier career as a
student. But it is the director himself, albeit a good Catholic,
who reminds her of the basic facts of the class struggle: yes, it
is *in their own interest* that employers step up production as

much as they can and at the lowest cost, and demand the greatest possible amount of work for the smallest salaries. So that if someone tries to put a spoke in the wheel, he will find himself up against these employers. This director was, of course, goaded to fury by the *naïveté* of this ex-student.

She does not immediately draw the inevitable conclusion from this; which is, I fear, that there is no valid solution within the framework of the system. But in fact she reveals this more clearly than she might have done had she reasoned it out. Stubbornly she perseveres with her demands, and takes part in a trade-union congress; her reward is not long in coming: at the first opportunity her benevolent employers give her the sack. She is taken back again afterwards, but she has lost the rights of seniority and can no longer be a delegate. It was an underhanded, but quite obvious punishment. From then on her head is filled with projects of revolt. And sometime later, sickened and defeated, she leaves her job. Some friends offer her work for which her knowledge is required; she becomes an intellectual again and is once more on the other side of the fence. "So you've given us up," says Ambrosine, one of her friends. And that is the final word.

This way out was open to her only because she had been a student, because she was no longer, properly speaking, a worker; the ending may seem therefore to limit the scope of her experience, and turn it, in spite of everything, into an "experiment"—a word the author hates, and which she is quite right to hate in this context. For you know before you start on it that an experiment will come to an end, and that you can get out of it alive, which alone is enough to differentiate it from a state of oppression in one of its most essential features: that of despair. From time to time a student, a priest, or an intellectual (such as Simone Weil) will decide to go and take a look. But, as I say, it is always and only by way of an experiment, a simulated experience in other words, which from start to finish depends on the subject's continuing desire to go through with it. Worker-priests can always stop being workers, without ever ceasing to be priests; sooner or later the intellectual returns to his books, and the student, even if he has been forced to earn his living, knows that in the end he will be a *cadre* and find his place in a privileged class of people. Such is the story of Daniel, the heroine's friend, who comes to see her one day abruptly transformed into "the well-born young man, his eyes cold and dead." In the course of time the same thing happens to the author. The worker, on the other hand, cannot solve his problems by exchanging one way of life for another, and scarcely has a hope of seeing the end of his daily torment. "It is finished, for me," says the heroine's mother; there is no way out.

Finally though, even the author's ambiguity is in a sense inevitable: for the heroine had to be able to escape to have strength and time enough to tell the story of the worker's life. She had to have learned the art of speech, or she would have remained dumb, like her companions in misfortune, and we should have known nothing. What is more, the ambiguity is here reduced to a minimum. The heroine of the story did not temporarily return to the way of life to which she was born just to fill her purse, or acting on a momentary impulse of generosity. She seriously planned to return where she belonged. And if she left that life again, it was because it really is intolerable. That is the reason why *Une Société anonyme* is the most sincere and honest testimony of working-class life today.

(*Translated by Jane Brooks*)

(Preface to *Un noir a quitté le fleuve*,
by Annie Lauran, Editeurs Français Reunis, Paris, 1968.)

11

The New Slaves

I

Sunday afternoon in a foreign city; the stores are closed, the
cafés deserted, the passers-by rare. Your heart burns with solitude—will you knock on one of the lighted windows, will you
grab the lapel of one of the fleeting passers-by and say: "Listen
to me. I come from far away but I am like you. Back there I
have friends, a family, I need warmth, friendship . . . !"

You know very well that that is impossible. You haven't yet
been driven to that point, these people owe you nothing, you
don't even know their language—just a few words, you would
lose their attention at the end of a few minutes. Furthermore,
could they really dispel your anxiety? No, it's useless; it's not
only the city that is foreign, it is you, above all, who is foreign,
separated by more than a windowpane, by more than a language. You're not a part of this city, you're out of your shell.

Imagine, in addition, that you are poor, badly dressed, even
perhaps dirty; you become a kind of permanent provocation,
you are, finally, a little more foreign. Be careful to seem most
anonymous, the most transparent possible. Avoid caressing the
head of a baby, avoid raising your voice, even with the most

The New Slaves

despicable people, avoid finding yourself alone with a woman in a deserted street, above all don't try to speak to one; there's a chance she'll run away shouting. Because that is a foreigner: he must be without face, without desires, without pride or else he might irritate, he might frighten.

If, finally, your skin is black! What can you do but avoid going out at all? When the daily work is done, once you've left the precise position behind the machine, go straight back to the collective hut, avoid placing before the others the troubling, disturbing problem of your existence among them. And if, one day, unbearably bored, you venture out all the same on a Sunday afternoon, in this foreign city, as did N'Diyae Seydou, the black hero of Annie Lauran's book, it's best to face the tunnel of the subway until the end of the trip. In such a way you will cross the city, the country, with your eyes closed, your soul closed, perhaps until the end of your exile.

Thirty-five thousand. There are 35,000 new black slaves in Paris.[1] I was watching those of Montreuil the other evening, seated on the ground in front of their huts, at the gates of the city, silent, distant, immobile, a few yards from the deafening, uninterrupted noise of the automobiles. There was an astonishing number massed together, like a brood of large black insects, gripped with terror before an extraordinary world, exuding an unbearable sadness, almost palpable, to the point of driving them mad. This is no fable; they sometimes do become mad. A blonde European friend of mine, who worked in Germany during the war, told me of this kind of sudden rage that can overcome a worker, and make him commit an insane act, destroy himself in order to begin the destruction of the world. Since it is impossible to live in this world, in this order of

[1] 35,000 salaried blacks in Paris; I have learned, in the meantime, from the film *El Salto*, that there are 350,000 Portuguese workers, and that, numbers aside, the problems are fundamentally the same. The blacks simply form an extreme case, a little more closed in, a little more beaten down, if that's possible.

things, let it perish with me: an infantile gesture, or a sublime one, like Samson bringing down the columns of the Temple, the act of a totally desperate slave: because foreign workers are indeed the slaves of modern times.

It's even worse than that. The slave used to belong to someone, to a man in any case. Of necessity, there entered into this relationship, beyond its basic iniquity, something fundamentally human. There is no man, I am convinced, even the most perverted Nazi, who doesn't try to justify his crimes to himself. This guilt at the heart of the human conscience is an enormous good fortune. Man strikes, wounds and kills, but he knows that he must explain this, first of all to himself. Then he quibbles, he at least speaks ironically, he reasons; this is the origin of a large number of ideologies: they are tortured pleas for the defense.

Now, these new black slaves, our slaves, are not the slaves of anyone in particular. That is to say, no one believes himself responsible for them. No one person is the direct cause of their abjection and their loneliness, no one person has relegated them to these huts and these hotels where they sleep twenty to a room, the same room in which they cook and even, sometimes, organize a sleep schedule, in rotation, for twenty-four hours. I have failed to write: Ridiculous: they are free. It is of their own free will that they live that way, rent those huts, organize their sleep time, so that they might send the largest amount of money possible to their country; they even prefer to group themselves in that way rather than live, eat, sleep, and die sometimes, each on his own.

I remember my shocked bewilderment when one of my Tunisian colleagues, a professor and a good man, calmly announced to me that he was going to the south to find a black woman for one of his slaves. Now, at a distance, I can almost admire the logic of the old system, by comparison, its adaptation to what became a familiar oppression. Since there were slaves, and one used them, it was necessary to look after their

The New Slaves

lives, at least their elementary needs, and if one of them was of the age to take a wife, it was necessary to get one for him.

Who worries about the broken families of our slaves, about their wives, young or old, who remain alone for years and who end up in despair? Who worries about their children who die— their fathers not even having seen them grow up and whose death is learned about through a clumsy letter written by a local merchant? We are legitimately horrified by the slavery which still is a practice in Arab countries, and even, I'm told, in Ethiopia. We must denounce it regularly and without let-up, and fight it more seriously than by means of an annual motion at the U.N.—because the whole world has become one and we can allow no such outrage on any part of the planet. But that should not prevent us from recognizing that from which we benefit, nor above all from seeing in it the identical meaning: that of the same ignominious trait of our own, always the same throughout history up till our own time, less cynical on the surface today but nonetheless unjust and lucrative.

It is always basically the same thing we are dealing with, through the variable figures of the slave and throughout all time. It would be interesting to figure out exactly, as can be done today, the cost of a slave and his yield; one would understand more clearly what slavery and its transformations are, and toward what they irresistibly tend. Quite simply, this slavery which continues, which is reborn in our cities, is, in our eyes, more troublesome in certain forms, less directly and overtly cruel, as we ourselves have, on the surface, become, but it always adheres to certain old, fundamental mechanisms. Thus the colonized of the French colonies resembled in many ways their colonizers; they cited the French revolution and aspired, as a prestigious honor, to speak French and to work as a mailman or a customs official, just as any average Frenchman does; so the colonized of the British colonies chose their leaders from among those graduated from Oxford and agreed, in spite of everything, to remain faithful subjects of her Majesty. This was because French colonialism was petit bourgeois and British was moralistic and cultural in ambition. Our own slaves are the slaves of what is called the industrial age, that is to say that phase of capitalism in which the breaking up of the ranks of the middle class will perhaps reach its maximum, where correlatively, the solitude of the individual and his abandon before the monster will be more and more appalling. So, our black slaves are the best illustration of the solitude and abandon and dispersion of each of us.

Isn't it already symptomatic that this industrial society uses so many foreigners so prodigiously? Clearer still, how can one not see that in some way it tends to change the maximum number of workers into foreigners? Thanks to what is delicately called *social mobility,* and what is actually a forced displacement of populations, that is to say an uprooting of all that makes up the thread of their lives, their natural and human surroundings. Slavery in the past was paternalistic, ours is anonymous and crushes the entire personality of the slaves, whose frame of reference, attachments and values are exploded.

II

This is why I believe one can accept only to a certain extent the comparison, fashionable nowadays, of the condition of the foreign worker to that of the proletariat. Foreign workers would quite simply be a new proletariat; they would have replaced our workers. The idea of the proletariat would thus be in a phase of evolution; one would extend it to peoples and not merely limit it to social classes. The relationship is clear, and perhaps a certain extension of the concept of the proletariat would be useful. However, I am not at all convinced that we can *confuse* these different images of the oppressed. Not to mention that I suspect there is too great a comfort in that; it is not a widening, an enlargement; it is a drowning. We begin by changing the emphasis from the proletariat to the foreign worker; then we pretend to forget the proletariat completely; from then on the real proletariat are the others, the foreigners; we no longer have a proletariat, there remain only masters.

Let us remember that an analogous demonstration had been tried apropos the colonized; the colonial relationship was only thought to be a simple one of dependence and economic exploitation. We know the consequences of this; we neglected at that point the other aspects of colonization, not realizing that the liberation would be first of all a national one. But, perhaps, there too we did not want to see that we were dealing with a specific phenomenon: the demands of an entire people against another people. . . .

If we need further proof, it would be enough to note that the trade unions hardly defend these new proletariat, black or not; they are of course wrong in the over-all perspective of universal solidarity of all oppressed. But this means too that they do not recognize them at once as completely similar to themselves. And we must admit that they are not completely wrong, because their aspirations, conduct and conditions are not identical. Now, if it weren't necessary to be very cautious in these areas, I would gladly propose the following law: *There is effective solidarity among the oppressed only when their objective conditions do not differ greatly.*

And if, moreover, there were a conflict, even a surface one, in their interests. We saw this during the Algerian war, during which the French trade unions were more than hesitant; we see it in the Jewish-Arab conflict, alas; and it doesn't seem that American unions are troubled by a war of genocide, against the unfortunate Vietnamese, in the name of American civilization. Now it is true that the black workers, and in a more general way, the foreign workers, do not identify themselves with the nation that employs them. But how could they when they are treated like subhumans, excluded, rejected and scorned by

THE PROLETARIAT

even the poorest? Even worse, they interfere with the laws of the only solidarity that could be offered to them: that of their fellow workers. They never participate in any demand; on the contrary, by their submission, they conduct themselves like strike breakers, they endanger union solidarity, allow themselves to be used by the bosses, accept all extra hours, agree to work under any conditions whatsoever. But how could they be combative, when they are so much more fragile, when they can be thrown out without explanation, expelled in forty-eight hours? Why wouldn't they be overanxious to get any sum of money whatsoever, when they came just for that and suffer exile and misery to send the largest possible amount home? It is true that they are afraid, that they are obsessed by their earnings. It is true that they are painfully humble, flexible and resigned; for a long time they have disappeared into the European proletariat. But isn't it for just that reason that they were made to come? Bourgeois housewives have rediscovered the pleasure of commanding with the Spanish and Portuguese maids.

In any case, whether it be a profound distinction or one of degree, the foreign worker is infinitely poorer, more alienated and more essentially proletariat than the others. Of course, all contemporary oppressed peoples are more or less affected in all their dimensions, all proletariat are relatively excluded from the dominant culture, or at least subtly separated, because nothing prepares them for it. It passes over their head, because the theater, museums, painting, music, present-day thought all are unintelligible to him. But in this case the exclusion is more complete, the separation more hermetic, since in addition we are dealing with another culture, and sometimes even another religion. Even participation in the most material forms, the most everyday of the cultural environment, risks to be affected. Often black workers can't even go around alone;[1] moreover they take a single subway line, always the same ride during

[1] An example cited by Annie Lauran.

which time they thus feel secure; away from that, removed from that rigid behavior, fixed once and for all, they panic, as neurotics. But how would we react in a tropical forest? We would probably use one path, panicked with the fear of losing our way.

Out of modesty, Annie Lauran has remained in the background, behind her hero, so that he would not be made to say more than he actually said, anything beyond that which he clearly understood of his condition. This is, of course, a modern approach, but the apparent humility of Annie Lauran should not delude us. This prudence is the guarantee of the authenticity and the profound truth of the experience, the results of which she transcribes for us.[1] She wants to suggest what the black worker in Europe today—and by extension perhaps the foreign worker—feels, thinks and experiences. Now, when she *chooses* in the daily observations of N'Diyae this simple remark: "At Golmy, under the trees, there are always red and yellow leaves and flowers, even in winter"—she translates, better than by a long development, his chilly sadness in this country of exile where the plants lose their foliage in winter, and his nostalgia for another place, the only one in which he can live without this permanent malaise. It seems to me, in short, that the author reaches her goal perfectly and that, when we have finished the book, we can understand from then on N'Diyae

[1] This effort, I feel, contained a certain ambiguity and a great deal of useless humility. In an effort to be faithful, in an attempt to come as close as possible to the actual expression, it was decided to leave the word solely to the protagonists. With or without a tape recorder, one sets out to note precisely what the subject says. Only it is the point at which literature is reduced to zero, since there is neither art nor even craftsmanship in such a step. Or at least it would be canceled out, if it didn't take such efforts, after the interview, to make this pile of illegible notes presentable; to put it another way, the matter of selection must come into it. Choice is, in my opinion, the second criterion of the work of art, if not the first, which would be perhaps invention: and furthermore, the role of invention can be slight, the severity of selection remaining necessary.

THE PROLETARIAT

and his comrades, we know who these furtive shadows embody, their despair and their modest pleasures, how they are sick and how they die, resigned, asking only to remain in the communal hut, until the last breath, surrounded by their own and not in the double exile of the hospital.

III

There remains the solution. This is what is always, wrongly, expected of the author: all right, what is the solution? Do you hesitate, are you embarrassed? You see. Will you give one with which the reader does not agree? That proves that your description was false. Can't one, however, analyze a misfortune and conclude, in despair, that one doesn't really know how to respond to it?

Is it nonetheless necessary to try?

Of course, one could ask for more kindness from the new masters, ask them to give better living conditions to their foreign slaves: that is to say, make less profit from them. That said, all we can do is shrug our shoulders: where have you ever seen the privileged, on their own, give up a part of their profit? In the name of what? Even if one could show them that it was to their own interest! For example, to show them that it's never good to have such a mass of ill-fed, ill-cared-for slaves; that they are the centers of disease and of contagion; that they exert a kind of stifled discomfort on the entire social body, xenophobia, racism, that they compromise the health and the over-all balance of the common society. Because there is, all the same, a common society between oppressor and oppressed, and I firmly believe it: the oppressors always pay a price for their oppression, even if they gain from it on the whole.

Failing in the matter of interest, one could ask them in the name of simple charity. I am not among those who condemn the little relief, even temporary, of charity in the name of the complete but distant cure. I've been told that in some town,

Rouen I believe, a kind of village was built, a kind of community in which the foreign workers found themselves among their own kind, without the overcrowding, the total absence of hygiene and the exploitation of landlords. Let us be very grateful for these acts of good will. It is to be hoped, of course, that the state would encourage them, would aid them financially in a task which is not natural to private individuals.

But the true end of the misfortune of the oppressed can only come from himself: *the underdeveloped countries must themselves stop relying on what seems an easy solution*—that is, the export of men. It brings in money, without preliminary investment: but this bleeding of men, the youngest, the most vigorous, the healthiest—isn't this investment basically lost? And what good is independence if, as soon as they are the new citizens of a free country, they can only live by leaving that country to enter into a new condition of servitude? Isn't it also true that this continual bleeding would also be a way of removing a surplus of unsatisfied and disturbed men who could put the established regime in danger? Of course, the utilization of foreign workers is the last form of the exploitation of man, of the permanent voracity of the capitalist system, of the permanent inequity of Western society. But it must be added that if it is prolonged, it will also be the explosive sign of the failure of the poor countries, of their crowded demography, of their political instability, of an artificial economy, and finally of their inability to make their country inhabitable. For the health of the poor countries, for their dignity as well, they must stop encouraging this.

I know very well that I am going to seem once more unrealistic. Since advanced industrial societies need a great labor force, and since underdeveloped countries ask for nothing better than to export the overflow of their population, how can one even suggest that this exchange be stopped, when it seems to be profitable to both parties? With which both are, at least, in agreement? "Come on, they're very happy to find work again

THE PROLETARIAT

with you." And it's true that the ex-colonizers have something
to sneer about. After so long a humiliation, sometimes bloody
defiance, and finally a victorious revolt, one would have
thought the ex-colonized would make it a point of honor not to
take up service again in the house of his former master. However, he does all he can to fool the customs men and fraudu-
lently pass the frontier he could, but a short time ago, pass
legally. The government of Algiers, the result of the most violent of colonial wars up until the time of Vietnam, calls for the
"free circulation of men," as if the French were dying to go to
work in Algeria. So be it. Let's say, for the moment, that I am
talking nonsense, that misery excuses everything: Joseph was,
of course, sold by his brothers on the occasion of a famine.

At least, let the meaning and price of this exchange of flesh
and blood be seen. Capitalism has needed, in its first period, in
order to grow and affirm itself, to sacrifice literally multitudes
of men, women and children. It is thanks to this merciless exploitation, in part at least, that it was able to form those re-
serves of wealth which constitute its present power. Today it is
perhaps necessary to its development that it use millions of
"foreign" workers. The workers sacrificed in the first industrial
period were equally "very happy" to accept, so as not to die of
hunger, the dreadful tasks offered to them, the miserable salaries, the fourteen-hour days, to offer up as a sacrifice their children (which is still done today in the mines). The workers
from the underdeveloped countries are today "very happy" to
find work in industrialized countries, under any conditions,
without lodging, without protection either from unions or the
law. They are the last to be hired, the first thrown out, always
at the bottom of the economic, social and professional scale.
But they collapse as well, from nostalgia and misery, from injustice and sickness, without counting the damage suffered by
their countries of origin. From this stems the enormous new
resentment which builds up between the rich countries and the
poor ones. Isn't this an historic conjunction analogous to that

from which Marxism was born? That is to say, the most violent
philosophy of resentment since the first Christianity and one of
the most powerful destructive ferments of Western society.
And already, in effect, a kind of new philosophy of revolt is
formed, which sets people against people, just as Marxism set
class against class.

Perhaps we can do nothing because it is an irreversible dy-
namics that leads us along. Perhaps collective life is nourished
by conflicts just as individual life is profoundly conflictual. But
if one day, finally ready to raise the moral standards of human
relations, we decided to conduct our community affairs equit-
ably and reasonably, it would be necessary to arrive at rights
and a morality which are actually universal: that is to say, to
consider the entire planet as really a single society. At once, it
would no longer be tolerable under any pretext whatsoever,
any alibi, that any human group be sacrificed to the interests of
another. Of course we are terribly far from such a fabulous step
forward for humanity. But couldn't the procedure be at least
set into motion?

How? It might seem that I am passing from one utopia to
another, hardly less formidable: the foreign worker, I have
said, is not simply a protelariat. I am not far from believing
that the foreigner, when he is not protected by his economic
power, is still *totally oppressed*. Couldn't we at least suppress
this doubling of misery, this two-staged burden of the foreign
worker? By making him simply a proletariat like the others?
This is why, also, I find it fallacious to confuse him with the
proletariat. Let us then stop performing this reduction in
thought to employ it concretely. He would gain so much from
it. It would be such a victory to make a simple worker of him,
with the same rights and duties. *To sum up, he would have to
cease being a foreigner.*

This is perhaps a very far-off utopia, and I propose it with a
certain degree of despair. But it is all the same a utopia which
can be more easily suggested because it does speak clearly to

the imagination of any man. It would be enough to ask him: "You yourself, have you ever been a foreigner? Do you think you might ever be one?" Then he would discover that we are all, permanently, potential foreigners. It would be enough to remind him that humiliation, suffering and revolt are in differing degrees, under different forms, the fate of the large majority among us, so that he might understand what this is all about. Remember that you were a slave in Egypt. Then he will admit that the treatment inflicted upon a foreigner is a result of a conception, still barbarous and primitive, of human relationships, which authorizes taking advantage of a position of strength.

(*Translated by Howard Greenfeld*)

V

THE
WOMAN

(This text was written, with the aid of C. Dubach-Memmi, in 1966, based on notes taken in 1963.)

12

A Tyrant's Plea

I

I hope that all I am about to say will be treated as highly suspect: for the first time in my life I am on the wrong side of the fence; in talking about women, I observe, with embarrassment and a touch of malice, that this time I am to be counted among the oppressors. I have already had to ask for a vote of confidence when on the subject of the French colonizers in Tunisia; I had too many friends among them, but I was, after all, objectively on the other side. This time there are no two ways about it: I am a man and have set myself up to investigate the emancipation of woman. How can I possibly make a sound judgment on a campaign undertaken against me? I shall surely be tempted to attenuate, and to find excuses for such convenient privileges as are mine. Further: this subject, the relationship between man and woman, depends on so many other hidden factors, that I desire to be suspected in advance of every imaginable ruse. In fact, I am perhaps at this moment trying out an even subtler trick, denouncing my own duplicity only that it may the better succeed. I must not go on or I will never finish. But at least I will have put my reader on his guard. Now it is up to him to figure out this problem for himself, as I try to do.

Today the whole outline of Simone de Beauvoir's feminist project is clear; it is certainly the most important ever to have been attempted. In the first volume of *The Second Sex* she defines woman as an oppressed creature and describes this oppression; in the second volume she proposes a theoretical solution for this real state of affairs; and in her memoirs she provides an illustration of her solution in the story of her own life. We move from theory to empirical proof, and we are dealing with a whole whose component parts are, first, a demonstration and, second, supporting documentary evidence. Thus this aspect of Simone de Beauvoir's work, which will probably find a permanent place in the history of ideas, reveals its essential unity as the story of a single journey: one woman's journey towards real emancipation.

A lot of discussion could have been avoided if critics had considered what she was attempting as a whole. The first criticism and the most strongly supported would then appear pointless: this experience of Simone de Beauvoir's, it has been said, is the concern of the author alone; it is too individual to be of any use to any other woman. Yet Simone de Beauvoir has answered this objection herself, at least in part, in *Force of Circumstance:* "Consideration of a particular case teaches one more than general and abstract solutions." I should like to add that any literary undertaking loses all its value unless this is true; for writing is never anything else but the communication of individual experience. Of course, to be allowed to draw general conclusions one must compare and contrast several experiences, the particular narrative being only a part included in the general reflection. But it is obvious that this experience is, nevertheless, *irreplaceable.* That without an inventory of concrete particulars no general conclusion has any reality.

In short, I believe that the central interest of Simone de Beauvoir's progress is just this: her clear exposition, as corroboration for her theoretical investigation, of an experience—her own, the only kind of experience one can finally be sure of. Valid discussion of her work should use her experience as a starting point. We must begin by asking if the solution to the problem raised in *The Second Sex*, which she proposes and has in fact applied to her own life, is a satisfactory one; and if it provides an answer to the difficulties of woman's existence as described there.

We must remove another false objection: the last sentence of her latest book is by now famous: "It was with astonishment that I realized the extent to which I had been cheated." There has been endless quibbling about this; countless ironic comments have been made on her conclusion, despite the frankness with which it is offered to the reader. So there is the brilliant result of a life-long struggle waged beneath the banner of existentialist liberty: an admission of failure, coupled with disillusion.

It is quite clear, however, to anyone who reads with a modicum of attention and good-will—an essential factor to understanding—that this is a failure neither of doctrine nor of experience. The author is in no way complaining of an individual hardship, resulting from the way of life she has chosen, but of a general misfortune inherent in every human existence: hers is a metaphysical observation. It is only thoughtlessly that one could use it as a weapon against her; even if I am wrong, at this level of reflection what life can we call a success, and what life a failure? Who could assert with conviction that his own was one or the other?

The outstanding feature of these memoirs is, on the contrary, their constantly triumphant progression, their affirmation, at all events, of a fixed certitude: here then, the author proclaims, is the life I have led in the light of an idea adopted very early in my career; I regret nothing, for I have accomplished my pro-

THE WOMAN

gram. While remaining faithful to myself I have been able to take what the world could offer. That alone is, in my opinion, a fine thing, to dare to conclude one's life thus. If there were an element of failure in this enterprise of Simone de Beauvoir's, it should be looked for elsewhere. But, from the outset, it is a successful struggle that is offered for our judgment by this author, in this work. Simone de Beauvoir, a woman, and therefore oppressed, has, she would have us believe, successfully brought about her emancipation; rightly or wrongly, honestly or by cheating a little, with lucidity or perhaps herself somewhat baffled, she believes in her victory. It is our job to weigh what this victory is worth; what is the meaning of this emancipation and at what cost is it achieved. In other words whether this liberation really leads to freedom.

Let us examine one last misjudgment of the work. Clearly the whole of these three large volumes, running to over 1,500 pages, is not concerned with this one aspect. They take the reader over the whole world, and through sixty years of a well-filled life; and in addition to the story of this life, they relate the annals of an epoch, and of a whole class of society. Thus, the emphasis placed afterwards on this campaign for emancipation, and on the importance given to Jean-Paul Sartre in this complex affair, irritates some critics by its exaggeration. More emphatically than in the case of the other two objections, I say that this is sheer stupidity. One can never from a single viewpoint embrace a whole life, nor for that matter a whole work of art; but it is not possible either to demand everything from a life, or a work, at once. Simone de Beauvoir chose to orientate her life in this particular way and to give us the story of it seen from this angle; she had a perfect right to do so.

Her decision was not, moreover, purely a question of convention. As I read her work I was convinced that she really had considered the meaning of her life to be such and had brought all her actions into line with this belief. Her work as a writer—which is the most important part of her—had really become the tool she used to free herself, as well as the account she renders of that liberation. Furthermore, this emancipation of a woman, as such, was brought about all along the line by means of her dialogue with one man, Jean-Paul Sartre. Her social and historical memoirs are after all built upon the private memoirs of the couple they formed. I believe her to be wholly sincere when she says: "In my life there has been one sure success: my relationship with Sartre." This must be the starting point for an analysis of her work: did the couple Sartre-Simone de Beauvoir provide a workable solution to the oppression of the individual woman Simone de Beauvoir, and can it in a general way serve as a model solution to the oppression of the female sex as a whole?

Readers will understand that, far from reproaching the author with making use of a particular instance, we intend to follow her example. Far from quarreling with her scheme, we shall instead inquire into whether she actually put it into practice in the manner she proposes.

It is only thus, by adopting the writer's own standpoint, that we can claim any right to question the legitimacy of her conclusions. Only then may we ask whether the experience described has really been taken to the limits to which the writer asserts she is leading us, and in consequence, whether it provides that bridge from the particular to the universal which does in fact distinguish all truly great ventures and great works.

II

The publication of an autobiography is probably always a bad move on the part of a writer. If he is wholeheartedly honest, he exposes himself irrevocably; without the comfortable disguise of fiction he cannot escape swift condemnation. If, with a different kind of honesty, he warns us that he is not telling us the whole truth, he will immediately be suspected of hiding the most important elements, and then contemptuously rejected.

THE WOMAN

Why announce an autobiography if one intends to omit what is most significant? Understandably he is tempted to cheat, to be only half sincere. Then once more, why an autobiography? To tell the truth, I can see only one solitary justification for this literary genre: that it should be a kind of supreme hoax, the author feigning absolute sincerity the better to divert the reader's attention and prevent him snooping elsewhere. In this way, fortunately, autobiography continues to hold its place in literature.

If Simone de Beauvoir will forgive me, the point I am trying to make is this: given the decided impossibility of full guaranteed sincerity in any art, we are obliged to ask the question: "Are we being told everything?" Or, aside from what is being revealed to us, what is the writer concealing? All the more so in this case where we are warned in so many words: "It is impossible to tell *everything*" (author's own italics). "I have consented in this book to certain omissions." Admittedly, she assures us that these gaps are of little importance, they are "omissions, never lies," a question of tact where living persons are concerned. But is the author, from the outset so committed, really the best judge of this? Who can guarantee that what is passed over in silence is not essential evidence for the file?

Here at hand is an example crying out for attention: how can one avoid speaking of their sexual relationship when considering a couple? Whatever one's embarrassment in trespassing on this peculiarly private aspect of the lives of couples in the public eye (I have in mind also Aragon and Elsa Triolet), it is impossible to neglect this side of things if one really wishes to understand the whole. It may be objected that that is entirely their concern; that it is in no way part of their work, which alone is being submitted to our judgment. But it is a false objection, since they themselves are offering us their individuality; since there is constant reference to this in their works; and since by their works they invite us to draw from it a lesson of universal relevance. To be over-modest in dealing with Simone de Beauvoir's works is even more pointless, considering that *The Second Sex* is the most courageous venture ever success-fully concluded by a woman on the subject of woman's sexual-ity, and by extension of that of the couple. Yet we are told nothing, or scarcely anything, of the sexual relations of this par-ticular couple; just what should be used as an illustration of the sexual relations of couples in general. Curiously enough, the poet Aragon reveals far more of this aspect to us, through images and symbols, than the minutely detailed memoirs of Simone de Beauvoir. We do not know whether their relations were harmonious; we do not even know whether they had sex-ual relations.

In *The Mandarins,* after meeting a man, the heroine tells us that she had rediscovered "that she had a body." Though we should beware of confusing an author and his characters, it has been too great a temptation to class this remark among the real-life facts that serve as a basis of the most fictitious works. It is well-known that the book was dedicated to the writer Nelson Algren. Now in *Force of Circumstance* we find confirmation of the fact that the Algren episode had been used, with only slight modification, in *The Mandarins.* Similarly, there is an obvious parallel between Beauvoir-Sartre and Anne-Dubreuilh. The fictional couple is not an exact copy of the real, but the intimate truth of their relationship is probably the same: the woman's sexual life is lived with the American writer, her daily life with the French philosopher, who also has his own sexual life else-where. The following words escape from Simone de Beauvoir's pen, apropos of Sartre's liaison with a certain M: "I often won-dered if he did not care more for M than for me . . . Accord-ing to what he told me, M shared completely in his reactions, his emotions, his desires . . . was this perhaps the sign of a profound harmony between them—a harmony at the very well-spring of life, present in the rhythm of its ebb and flow—that Sartre did not sense with me, and which was more precious to him than our understanding?"

THE WOMAN

What is this "very well-spring of life" and "the rhythm of its ebb and flow" for an author as little given to lyricism as Simone de Beauvoir, if not a reference to sexual life?

If critics maintain, in spite of everything, that I am over-interpreting, that my explanation is unfounded, the fault is perhaps not my own. If the writer of these memoirs of the life of a couple does not herself furnish us with more details on the subject, we are effectively reduced to reading between the lines. And again, if they complain that this business is not really so very important, I shall repeat that they are not playing fair. How can you pretend that it is not important for the understanding of the relationship between a man and a woman to know whether they sleep together? It would be even more misguided in such a philosophy as that of Simone de Beauvoir to assert that the precise nature of their physical rapports, particularly in the case of a couple, is without significance. Perhaps the most that can be said is that the conclusion usually drawn is not the right one; and that two people can form a perfect couple, while their physical lives remain separate. But in that case the question should have been more clearly stated: whether this is the kind of man-woman relationship which provides the true solution to the oppression of woman by man within the couple.

We might have been more firmly convinced by a few pieces of supporting evidence: a condemnation of jealousy, for example. It will be remembered how violently Sartre reacted to the journalist Maria Craipeau who, in a review of *Force of Circumstance*, marveled at this absence of jealousy (on which point she was, however, mistaken). Sartre replied that he found that sentiment odious (on which point he was certainly not wrong). But the journalist was perhaps justified in asking whether passion could exist without jealousy. I must admit that Sartre's rage leaves me puzzled: what was it that she had wounded in him that was so delicate, so beset with problems that he could not bear it to be questioned? And why did not

Simone de Beauvoir defend herself? In view of Sartre's agitation, one may well ask oneself if Maria Craipeau, so brilliantly crushed by the great writer, had not in fact touched on a sore point: namely, the very definition of the couple, on which their alliance was poised in a painfully achieved and ever-threatened state of balance.

Jealousy is an out-moded sentiment: so say the great minds of both right and left wing, oddly enough in agreement on this point. It is a sequel of the male's former economic domination of the female. A man is prone to jealousy because he considers his wife as his property, as his possession; he allows no one to touch her. He, however, would like to get at other people's property; and if, all the same, he feels guilty about this, it is precisely because he thinks he is infringing on another's proprietary rights. Certainly something of that is to be found in jealousy, for there is a bit of everything in all human behavior. But I do not think it is necessarily the essence of that passion. I have seen children, their faces literally twisted by the pain of jealousy, and not always jealousy of younger brothers and sisters. And women know jealousy also, even if they do not always play a directly active part in this economic rivalry. In any case, even if the roots of jealousy are to be found in frustrated ownership, it is still rather the psychologist's business than the economist's, simply because we are dealing with a sentiment, an emotion, a passion. I am, however, prone to believe that it springs from an even more fundamental desire: the need for security, felt probably by every creature all his life, and to which is linked, too, the famous mother-complex. A woman who goes with another man *abandons* the first (the reverse is true, too, of course) and *betrays* him; these terms are not merely metaphorical, but literally true. It is clear moreover, that this abandonment and this betrayal are felt more deeply as such if an understanding had existed between the man and the woman and each had sought refuge in the other.

This is just one more aspect of the couple phenomenon. Yet

THE WOMAN

again, the relationship of the couple is also a substitute for the
security, the undeniable warmth and confidence which human
beings receive from their parents and which they defend by
jealousy, by aggression and even by crime, if need be. When it
is suggested that Simone de Beauvoir's attachment to Sartre is
reminiscent of a girl's affection for her father, she is wrong to
be offended, and the public is wrong to sneer. It is certainly a
far-reaching observation, and this aspect of the couple requires
close investigation, both in the case of the couple we are dealing with at present, and of all couples. Above all, it must not be
thought that the couple relationship is a simple one: a man and
a woman bound by some obvious contract. Nor that such and
such a partial remedy—an improvement in their economic relations, for instance—is going to be enough to cure the troubles
of all couples, and institute once and for all the ideal man-
woman relationship. But I shall return to this point later. At
present I simply want to add that this need for security is not in
itself a defect in the human animal, any more than is the need
to possess, if it exists. They are both harmful only when they
lead to oppression. In a general way I am not far from the
opinion of the journalist, and the opinion of most people, that
no passion exists without jealousy, that is without anxiety and
suffering.

An even stranger example is that Simone de Beauvoir accepts
and attempts to justify the absence of children in her life. It
had been observed with regard to *The Second Sex* that children
were accorded scant attention in this theory of the emancipation of woman. In this life, presented to us as a pattern, they are
virtually ignored. Simone de Beauvoir scarcely speaks of them;
a line or two, a hint here and there, often making its appearance in spite of herself, like those nightmares—a knitting
needle in an egg yolk—that she professes not to understand,
but which are however quite plain. Once again, it will be said,
she was quite within her rights in not expatiating on that
theme, which is actually too intimate, and, one may suppose,

too disturbing for her. Certainly a child, or the absence of a child, signifies fear or desire of conception, of giving birth, of abortion, all the different kinds of guilt, that whole realm of strange biology, and all those unfamiliar events which a man finds such difficulty in imagining. But to sidestep all this in the enterprise under discussion is to throw doubt on its value as a prototype. How can one write of the couple without writing of children? The subject forces itself on the attention so that it cannot be ignored, and silence in that case is as eloquent as what is said; particularly when the writer is one whose pen is rarely still, and who talks often for the sheer pleasure of talking about herself.

But let me explain myself more clearly: here again, I am not simply summing up the criticisms that have been made of Simone de Beauvoir. I do not make a virtue of child-bearing, nor consider abstinence from it as worthy of blame. I do not look upon it as a duty, but as a right, more precisely, as *woman's right.* And, naturally, since one always has the power not to claim one's rights, no one should blame Simone de Beauvoir for not having wanted children in her life. One cannot help remarking, though, that in the context of this emancipation, of which she offers us a pattern, she could not or did not want to exercise her right. Everything concurs to make us feel that one of the constant conditions of success for this exemplary couple was that they should be childless (and once more I have Elsa and Louis Aragon in mind).

I do not believe, either, that Simone de Beauvoir can be charged with any inconsistency. On the contrary, I have been struck by the ultimate consistency of these two lives, which very early on were infused with the same purpose and came, in the end at least, to view themselves in one and the same light. Simone de Beauvoir discovers that the married woman is subject to the worst kind of oppression: an oppression permitted by law. In order not to fall a prey to this, she decides once and for all not to marry. And in fact she was to be

THE WOMAN

always legally and economically independent of Sartre, whatever linked them in other ways. Observing that a child is a weighty material, moral and metaphysical responsibility, she decides not to have children. Indeed, without family ties, the couple is free to travel, to go from country to country, from town to town, as they please. Unattached, and financially undemanding, they are relatively independent of history and of geography and even of the society in which they live.

But then we begin to doubt whether that state of affairs removes the dilemma. Or, more precisely, how it is removed and at what price. *The need to block all routes against oppression leads this particular couple towards a kind of abstraction.* Their interest in politics and the attitudes they adopt are almost always theoretical. It was not until the war in Algeria that Simone de Beauvoir witnessed a mass rising and discovered at that moment, with a surge of new emotion astounding at her age, the sensations of communion and of collective warmth. She was perfectly well aware of all this and admits to it, as always, with simplicity. She speaks of the *"de-reality"* of her life, and of Sartre's also, in spite of his efforts to combat it. In order to remain free, he does not marry, does not found a family, begets no children; in this he is consistent, and can more efficiently lead the life he has chosen: he can write what he will, and when he is in danger, at the time of the O.A.S. for example, he moves from his district, or goes to Italy; and he is perfectly right to do so. But the resulting personality is something rather abstract. What father of a family could so easily move, even from one apartment to another? As he becomes famous this unreal quality clings closer to him. He becomes untouchable, and at the same time his courage, though it cannot be denied, is less remarkable because he is risking so much less. Witness, for example, the story of the F.L.N. cases; no charge was filed against him despite his readiness to be inculpated.

And for a woman, however, there is something worse than

this somewhat unsubstantial liberty, which is perhaps after all the inevitable lot of any artist. If, as I believe, not to have children is, for a woman especially, a kind of self-mutilation, the candidate for freedom will find emancipation on these conditions set at too high a price. Is there only this choice left for the female half of these distinguished couples, the male half of which seems at last to be granting his companion complete equality, the choice between freedom and the sacrifice of an essential part of her nature? If I may use a phrase already employed in my account of the evolution of oppressed beings, I should say that in the case of Simone de Beauvoir we again find ourselves faced with a *self-rejection*. It is certainly only a partial self-rejection, since she has overcome her natural failings on so many scores, and has achieved what so many women are still deprived of. But she has to pay for her success by this one great privation; on one capital point she has to continue to reject herself. For to reject maternity is to reject one's essential femininity. And I think I have already proved sufficiently that to deny one's own nature is never a valid solution.

The proof of the foregoing is that Simone de Beauvoir cannot, on this score any more than on others, propose herself as an example. She cannot even trust herself to speak of it. Or if she does, she uses strangely involved and unconvincing arguments from one who had accustomed her readers to a self-imposed standard of scrupulous clarity. Critics of the male sex, she says, have blamed me for speaking of things I had no experience of. But they do so all the time, is her angry rejoinder. Why should I not have the right to speak of child-bearing? She does not see how she betrays herself the moment she opens her mouth. For on this problem she cannot compare herself to the opposite sex; nor could she give the only possible reply: I am a woman, and when I speak of children, I speak of what I know.

A comparison springs to mind which I will set down, for what it is worth. The Catholic Church has also offered us a pattern, of the ideal man; one to whom passion and procreation alike are denied: he is the priest. Is a free woman then also necessarily a woman without a partner and without children? To how many women might one present such an ideal, and with what hope of success? This is liberty at too high a price, above all of too rare a quality, ever to be subject to generalization.

III

In short, it is debatable whether this emancipation is really one at all. Unrivaled in her description of the oppression of women, Simone de Beauvoir fails, it appears, in trying to find a suitable way out. It is understandable that so many young women, even while admiring and respecting her work, should be reticent in their judgment of it; for she offers no solution to their main problem, which is how, in spite of everything, in spite of their impatience, in spite of the justice of their demands on men and on society as a whole, how to maintain the life of the couple.

Let me hasten to add that we are all extremely confused. Without a shadow of doubt, women have proclaimed their sexual, economic and political freedom; how is the ideal of the couple to weather the storm? We can hardly tell what the new ideal relations between man and woman should be, and we waver between irony, resignation and aggressiveness. Must we then assume that the death-blow has been dealt to the couple as such, and must we openly prophesy its imminent disappearance? Apparently, though, no one of either sex desires this. But is the couple presented to us by Simone de Beauvoir a true couple? A couple whose members do not make love, have no children, do not even live together? It is this last, I must admit, that impressed me most particularly, not for the mere fact of non-cohabitation, but for what that signifies: an absence of the daily need to see each other, to be assured of the other's physical existence. And this is proved by the fact that, after her awkward explanation of the various advantages of living separately, she goes to live with Lanzman. One may be tempted to think that she has renounced the above-mentioned advantages, or that there was something else between Lanzman and her more important than such trivial conveniences. And then there are those long months of separation. It is true she asserts that absence "does not frighten" her; at the least this suggests that it was not particularly agreeable to her. How many couples could be content with such a life? Happy in their *togetherness,* while traveling apart from each other and making love separately? How many couples could continue to survive, as *couples* let it be understood, and not the mere shadow of an association? How many couples and how many women would find here their fulfillment?

For fulfillment, surely, is the essential aim. We have been able to verify in the case of most other kinds of oppression, that revolt cannot be an end in itself; that at a certain moment the subject must strike out beyond that and form a new relationship with the world; that it was probably that moment that marked the end of "liberation" and the beginning of liberty. Through and beyond her revolt, over and above her denial of herself, woman must re-inform all the aspects of her being. Of course, it would be easy for Simone de Beauvoir to reply: "But how many women achieve fulfillment under the present conditions of cohabitation, child-bearing and faithfulness?" She is right, of course, but the problem set us is just that: women must be rescued from their present moral vacuum. I must reiterate too that there is no valid reason to criticize an author who observes the manifestations of oppression for limiting himself to their sole description. The solution is not always as evident as the weight of the injustice; crushed by oppression, one is often incapable of imagining what happens when the yoke is shaken off. Nevertheless, that moment does finally come, when denunciation of the oppressor or even active opposition is no longer enough, and when the most fitting remedy must be

THE WOMAN

found and applied, in order that the oppressed may recreate his personality.

It is for her very femininity that woman is oppressed, just as it is for his Negritude that the black man is persecuted and for his Jewishness that the Jew is victimized. The particular point at which oppression is concentrated on a woman is in her relations with men and with children. I need hardly repeat that woman is the victim of the whole of society too, and oppressed in all her acts. But all oppressed creatures are afflicted in some *specific* way which lies at the root of all their sufferings. In order most effectively to combat any particular oppression, one must first discover its distinguishing features. In order that their emancipation may be real, women must be considered as women: that is, as lovers and as mothers. For the liberation of the female sex, new relations must be established in the domain of love and of maternity.

When I speak of love here, let it be clearly understood that I do not only refer to mere sexual desire, which would be a simple question of give and take, the man and woman concerned finding equal satisfaction. I am thinking of a deeper, more firmly rooted sentiment, which is perhaps at the origin of the couple relationship, and not vice-versa, and by which the woman replaces the mother and prefigures the whole world; and I intend too the whole complex of exchanges and reciprocal needs between man and woman. A great deal of stress has been laid on the purely erotic emancipation of woman—and with justice. Those who pretend to see here nothing but claims of an obscene nature have misunderstood everything. Women have for centuries been starved of erotic satisfaction; it is normal therefore that they should attack this particular oppression. But subsequently, the whole of woman's love-life must be recreated, and, I might add, man's too. What a contemptible victory she would achieve if she restricted herself to an erotic revolt and thus definitively reduced the whole of love to this one aspect. No, our common problem is this: how to satisfy the need of woman for man and of man for woman, after sexual emancipation, and all the other kinds of emancipation?

If there were any need to stress the complexity of this problem, assuredly more intricate than Simone de Beauvoir's limpid phrases would lead us to suppose, we might find confirmation of it right here in her work. This, incidentally, is something that often happens in the case of works that are particularly rich in ideas: they escape the carefully meditated intentions of their authors. In spite of so much fine, bold inspiration, of a project so firmly mapped out, here is Simone de Beauvoir giving way to these awful, reactionary emotions. She is suffering! She is crying! She is jealous—positively ill with jealousy! Of Sartre we still know nothing, and we must wait for him to publish the rest of his autobiography in the hope that he will touch on these subjects. But Simone de Beauvoir is shattered every time she discovers that in some particular liaison Sartre is going rather far. In the case of his affair with M, for instance, despite the surprising brevity of the passages where she speaks of it, we can guess that this adventure must have been terrible for her, since for the first time (?) she calls in question the very nature of what binds her to the philosopher. On reflection the reader realizes with astonishment that all Simone de Beauvoir's writings center around the problem of the couple. What else is *She Came to Stay* but the story of a triangular relationship, where murder is perpetrated by the heroine on the person of her rival? The theme is resumed in *The Mandarins*, and stressed by being presented from two different points of view. It is more important still in the memoirs and in *The Second Sex*. A preoccupation so constant, vaguely labeled "the relation with the other," whereas it is almost always the opposite partner of a couple who is concerned, is clearer proof than any other of how dependent woman continues to be on man, even when that woman is Simone de Beauvoir.

We reach the point where we even wonder whether she ever seriously believed in the possibility of this "system" of perfect

THE WOMAN

mutual freedom, advocated by Sartre with respect to the couple, early in their association. When, apparently quite by chance, she enters upon a liaison with Algren, soon after the Sartre-M affair, it is impossible not to feel that she is taking her just revenge; and that if she alone had been involved, she would have remained faithful. With all her bravado, and all her determination, she ends, as usual, by telling us everything. A few veiled hints here and there give us to understand that in fact she would have sacrificed her independence if Sartre had required it of her; but "Sartre was not by vocation a monogamist"; that the trio was "an infernal arrangement"; that it was Sartre's own creation and that she was terrified by it; that in refusing to have children she was also afraid of infuriating Sartre who, she remarks oddly, would thereby have been forced to become adult; that she suspected Sartre's apparent candor, and lacked confidence in the possibility of mutual sincerity; and that she was full of resentment, yes, resentment, like every jealous, frustrated woman seeking revenge. It becomes positively embarrassing to hear her repeated insistence that Sartre is mad. If her constant reference to the one or two nervous attacks experienced by Sartre springs from her desire for truth, it is strange that she did not feel she should be guided here too by her famous "discretion." In her ingenuousness it is a long time before she realizes that the "system" has not functioned without "a certain amount of loss and damage, paid for by *the others*." She ends up facing once more even the old problem of faithfulness: "a problem which in *Force of Circumstance* I too readily imagined was solved: is there any possible compromise between fidelity and liberty, and at what price can it be achieved?" Unless I am mistaken, with this query all the rest is once more thrown in doubt; for her whole attitude here reveals passion, anxiety and jealousy.

Similarly with child-bearing, and I include here all the consequences of maternity: the existence of children, and all they demand in the way of time, energy, money and also affection. For, if we try to solve this fundamental problem of the female condition without taking all that into account, our solution will be purely theoretical and, which is worse, tend towards a kind of distortion.

To accept womanhood is to accept also maternity. The emancipation of woman certainly includes her liberation on the erotic plane, but the latter cannot be complete if it does not embrace the child, and is certainly incomplete if the child is excluded. If children are eliminated a conditional liberty alone is possible, one that is both falsified and curtailed. For a woman (and for a man too, though in a different way) to have children is perhaps as important psychologically and biologically as to have a love-life. The woman is only then whole and entire. To give women their freedom is *not,* as Simone de Beauvoir seems to suggest, to give them freedom from childbearing, but to liberate them within the context of their motherhood.

The problem is, how. For this purpose we must not shirk investigation into the details of domestic organization. I shall not undertake it here, because it is necessary to organize the whole of society with regard to the details of women's daily life. The reader should not shrug his shoulders at such a sweeping measure of reform. For, after all, women form more than the half of society, which up to now has always been conceived with the aim of satisfying the desires of the male sex. The principle of this reorganization is clear too: woman is exploited because of her function as a bearer of children. From now on men must be prevented from taking advantage of this state of affairs the better to lead their women by the nose.

I have, I think, indicated the particular bias to be given to the remedial measures applied to feminine oppression. If, on the contrary, steps are not taken in this direction, women will continue to define their status in terms of the requirements of the male, even if they refuse their natural functions, which means in fact being content with a negative definition of their status vis-à-vis the male sex. It is here that Simone de Beauvoir's real failure lies.

Her work sounds to us like a long shout of triumph, an account of her determined progress towards victorious emancipation. Her conflict with her own social milieu apart, as soon as she meets Sartre, and their pact is signed, freedom is potentially within her grasp. Everything becomes clear, coherent and even easy, in spite of the periodic crises. Her intention was to show how she became a free woman, and how any woman can be free. Her experience and her demonstration are of capital importance. Yet, when we put her three books down, we are left wondering whether we have witnessed a great defeat, disguised in the tattered folds of a torn banner. She asserts that between Sartre and herself there was the equal intercourse of two free creatures, each respectful of the other's liberty. Certainly, but to obtain this, *she* had had first to forgo the normal demands of *her* freedom.

We are now in a position to reply to the question asked of us. Simone de Beauvoir has lived a life of great cultural intensity, she has had a highly distinguished companion, wealth, literary and social success; but she has not succeeded in the common run of women's affairs. It is this which distinguishes woman from the rest of humanity, and in this domain that a solution is required. For reasons which she does not fully explain, she could not meet these requirements, because she could not, or would not, bear that yoke. In the end, Simone de Beauvoir has not explored to the limits her feminine individuality.

Incidentally—though this is an even more serious consideration—this failure supports a more general observation: it proves once again that men cannot escape oppression by their own unaided efforts; that in a collective state of oppression one can only achieve the false freedom of abstraction. Quite unexpectedly, Simone de Beauvoir gives us proof that woman cannot achieve emancipation so long as her relationship with the masculine world remains as it is. So long as these objective conditions continue to be imposed on women, that is to say, so long as the conditions imposed on love and on motherhood are not altered on a universal scale, I cannot see what new elements can be introduced into woman's life.

I am perhaps arguing from the man's point of view, and maybe covertly defending my own interests by demanding, like a demagogue, the maximum, in order not to concede a minimum. I have acknowledged that through the emancipation of woman I was also seeking the emancipation of man, and therefore that of the couple. This is because it does not seem to me possible, for the moment at least, to envisage any emancipation that is not founded on a new kind of association between man and woman; a change not only in the economic aspect of the association or in its institutions, but a total reform of the whole, passion included. I beg to remind the reader that I also warned him that the foregoing pages were likely to be no more than *a tyrant's plea.*

(*Translated by Jane Brooks*)

VI

THE
DOMESTIC
SERVANT

13

The Return of
the Pendulum

I

In a perfectly developed film, Harold Pinter and Joseph Losey's *The Servant,* a quick scene at the end comes as a surprise to a number of spectators: Susan, the fiancée of the master of the house, throws herself in the arms of Barrett, the valet. Nothing, according to them, prepared the way for such an action except, possibly, the atmosphere of the orgy that had taken place. Moreover, they wanted to see in it useless erotic excesses. Even better: the young woman hated the valet, and if she was perhaps disturbed by the presence of prostitutes and the bestial outburst of this scene, she still would not have thrown herself in the arms of her worst adversary. In short, one would have to believe that the authors not only showed a lack of taste, but that they commited an error. This would indeed be astonishing in the work of a director who is so aware of his goal, so intent in his means.

Unless this supposed negligence is just the contrary—a strong indication. And I would rather believe that it is charged with special intentions. This embrace between Susan and Barrett makes a point: the valet symbolically takes the woman of his master who had previously taken his. Thus, we have a symmetrical revenge. This is not all, and it is perhaps not the most important thing. Barrett had maneuvered everything so that his master would go to bed with a little maid, and this would be an unjustifiable vengeance. This master is not an evil brute; time and again he defends his servant against his fiancée; after firing him, he softens and takes him back; they play together like two adolescents, etc. In short, what the valet wants to get at more surely is the fiancée, it seems. She must be beaten, humiliated to death. By this embrace, Barrett finds himself exactly in the position of Tony; he replaces his master and dominates the woman, since it is understood that eroticism is a means of domination. To be sexually dominated by a valet is the greatest humiliation. The young woman makes no mistake about it. The scratching of the valet's face with a heavy bracelet, which ends the scene, is of murderous intent.

Why this pitiless duel? The conflict, by way of the master, between valet and fiancée, begins almost from the start of the film and soon becomes a desperate one. She endlessly gives him absurd jobs to do, changes the order which he puts into the house, openly suspects him of aiming at some contemptible goal by clinging to his charge; she ends up asking him to use a deodorant. In short, she uses all the admissible and inadmissible spitefulness of a situation of class domination. Now, at no particular time is Susan presented to us as particularly evil; why is she so stubbornly perverse towards Barrett? At the same time, one couldn't understand why the valet goes so far in his aggression if Losey didn't emphasize it so much. Why does he go so far as to drug his master, to literally destroy him after having mocked him in so many ways? Why is he so Machiavellian, when he seemed so correct in the beginning? Losey and Pinter carefully tell us that he had served in many houses from which he had brought excellent references. They show him as a man of many good qualities—careful, a good cook, a man who

loves his job. And he ends up organizing orgies with prostitutes, in the house he once directed with such care and respect!

Why, if not because the explanation of this behavior is not
found solely in the character of Barrett? Nor in that of Susan,
nor that of Tony? There too Losey multiplies the indications
and leaves us no doubts. The master is a pathetic boy, a lazy
teller of tales; he tells at the beginning of the film of how he
cleared a corner of the jungle. He is weak, someone who becomes too quickly a toy in the hands of the unchained valet,
who surely didn't deserve such a continual onslaught. Actually,
by this accumulation of significant detail, Losey wants to give
us one of the principal keys to this extraordinarily cruel film:
the behavior of each of the partners is not explained solely by
their characters, by their psychologies, but by the relationships
that will progressively tie them together. Susan, at first merely
jealous of the position the valet holds in the home of her fiancé,
where she one day hopes to reign, becomes the symbol of domestic oppression; Barrett, the perfect servant at the beginning
of the film, is transformed into a total revolt against his condition. Tony, the weakest link of the drama, will literally disinte-
grate in this confrontation. This desperate, destructive struggle
to a more or less symbolic death, to the destruction of the three
characters, is the result of the domestic relationship brought to
its culmination.

Through his master, the valet wants to avenge his humiliation by means of the woman. And since this humiliation was
systematic, he will apply to his unfortunate master the same
system; he will make him go through the same trials. And as
this humiliation was excessive, as the oppression reached an
unbearable limit, he will push his revenge to a hitherto unknown limit; as if it were necessary that the scales which were
weighed too heavily on one side had to be counterbalanced by
the same weight on the other side. He arranges it so that his
master goes to bed with a servant girl. In the perspective of
class the downfall has already begun. It isn't enough; the valet

THE DOMESTIC SERVANT

goes to bed with the servant girl too—she is probably a prostitute—he carefully tells this to his master and to his fiancée as
well. They will thus be, directly and unequivocally, affected in
their class values. The sexual dimension, which is in evidence
throughout the film, is obviously important here. But I don't
believe that it is at any point the final point of Losey and Pinter's story. On the contrary, all the erotic scenes have the same
meaning, in some way exterior to them: the transformation of
the habitual link between master and valet and its replacement
by its opposite. In the same way, the scabrous incident in the
bathroom in which the valet uses the bathtub and all the toilet
articles of his master. After the use of the same woman, these
objects extend the bodily promiscuity which is imposed on the
master. Curiously, this seems even worse: it is an attack on
such natural, everyday and in a way humble privileges that
only a particularly evil force would have attempted.

And, above all, Barrett, finally avenged, should have been
able to stop there, since he won, since he saw to it that the
fiancée, sickened, left his master and the house. But everything
happens as if nothing could satisfy him, as if the sending away
of Susan were merely one step, one phase, in an infinitely more
complex process, as if the mechanism, once set into motion, had
to run its full course. This course, contrary to the condition of
the domestic, is that of the degradation of the master; as if
from now on it would be necessary to make the master pay for
the totality of the servant's degradation, up to and including
the death of the master, just as the blow with the bracelet was
meant to provoke the death of the valet. As if it had to operate
until the final swing of the pendulum.

II

The Servant tells a relatively uncommon tale, in literature at
least if not in life: the destruction of a master by his servant.
Usually the opposite phenomenon is described, the growing

abjection of a domestic servant, without in any case placing enough emphasis on the close connection between the annihilation of the domestic and the behavior of the master. That is natural, since most of these descriptions are given by writers of the established order. The baseness of the domestic must not seem to be the result of the airs, contortions or ruses suffered under the yoke. On the contrary, the more the domestic is crushed, the more the master is justified. This is not surprising once one has understood the general phenomenon of the reversal of the accusation in all oppressive relationships.

However that may be, Genet's *The Maids, Les Abysses* by Vauthier and Papatakis, and the few pages already published by Dr. Le Guillant on the general household maid have made a great advance in the understanding of the domestic servant, in placing the servant in perspective. We now begin to be informed on what sometimes happens in the soul of a domestic, from the most harmless disturbances to the most serious perversions, including crime. We know furthermore that these authors have based their knowledge on actual cases, the most paroxysmal, thus the most illuminating, that of the Papin sisters, for example.[1] On the other hand, there has been very little said about the masters, who were somehow not a part of the drama; they were merely empty figures whom the domestics villainously attacked.

Here then, finally, actually face to face, for the first time in my knowledge, the two sides of this pathology of dependence: the growing disorders in the soul of the master this time as a consequence of the conflicting relationships with a domestic. We have already had the opportunity to bring to light an equivalent process in the colonizer-colonized relationship. An analogous range of feelings and behavior finds its meaning in a correlative range in the other partner. And it is the ensemble of

[1] The case of the Papin sisters who sadistically murdered their mistresses inspired Genet's *The Maids* and was widely discussed in France. (Editor's note.)

the drama which constitutes the colonial relationship or, in this case, the domestic relationship. Herein, I believe, lies the originality and importance of Pinter and Losey's film. It shows clearly how the deliberate destruction to the point of physical ruin of the master by his valet is the response to an excessive aggression on the part of the master. This is inevitable when domination reaches a certain point.

Susan begins by attacking Barrett professionally; she makes fun of his cooking and his gloves, the symbol of his functions. This is serious enough. Barrett the man is most careful about his professional role as valet. He is always correctly dressed, as a valet who accepts and affirms his position, in a black suit and white gloves; he is proud of having served aristocrats; he does what he should do, on his own, without being asked. In the winter, on his own initiative, he prepares hot foot baths for his master when he thinks the latter risks catching cold. By ferociously attacking Barrett as a valet, Susan really strikes out at the man as well, because the domestic servant is allowed little private life. He, more than other oppressed, tries to save himself through identification with his job; and if he is assailed, repudiated in this aspect of his personality, it is probable that he will feel even more threatened than other dominated men. But Susan doesn't even stop there, at this dangerous line; she pushes further ahead to the heart of Barrett's humanity. "Barrett, I don't give a damn what you think." "Barrett, do you use a deodorant?"

When certain limits have been reached, the oppression become literally unlivable, because the man himself is called to question: the valet, as all oppressed, must either accept this annihilation or else pass to the attack. This latter is what Barrett will do. Only, as Losey shows us, the valet too cannot set a limit to this natural reaction. Everything happens as if the pendulum, too far on one side, must go too far on the other.

At first, Barrett merely wants to drive out this abusive fiancée, who, not yet mistress of the house, already gives orders, replaces the master and mistreats the servant. He only defends himself. He brings into the house a strange creature—half maid half prostitute—whom he passes off as his sister and whose mission is to seduce Tony. She quickly succeeds in this. Then, Barrett sees to it that Susan knows that Tony, at the same time he is courting her, is sleeping with the maid. This is a profound humiliation for Susan; the couple is broken up. Of course, the servant is fired: but the fiancée also decides to leave. Bit by bit, the goal is achieved. So ends the first part of the film.

The work could have ended there; it would have been entitled *A Servant's Revenge*. Many spectators, who found the rest of the film superfluous, thought it was drawn out from this point on. In fact, they were somewhat bored because they didn't grasp the important meaning of the rest of the film. But it's probably no exaggeration to say that the real meaning of the film began here, that everything that preceded was only a preparation. At the least, the two parts form a whole, and it is the second part that achieves it, that gives it its fullness.

Some time after this double break, Tony, who has become a weak man, incapable of directing his own affairs, preferring to live in the imagination and who is now deprived of his two pillars, valet and fiancée, begins to drink. It is in this way that he meets his former valet in a bar. The latter play-acts a comedy of tenderness and easily has himself rehired. Here I think the most fascinating part of the film begins, a little slow, but necessarily so because it deals with the underhanded strategy used to undermine the unfortunate Tony. Barrett did not need to get back his old job with Tony, because in the meantime he had been able to find work elsewhere. His new job is not bad; he doesn't complain about it, he doesn't seem to lack money, he pays for the drinks without difficulty. He is in no way desperate. Then why did he want to go back to Tony? Here, homosexuality has been spoken of, of a sexual attraction between the

THE DOMESTIC SERVANT

two men. This probably is true, but it seems to me secondary. I'll come back to it in a moment. *But he returns to his former employer above all to complete his plan of destruction.*

It seems difficult, it's true, to explain why he so hounds Tony; at first, in any case. Barrett has been humiliated and sent away; but so has Susan. After such an outburst, Tony could hardly do otherwise; he plays his role of the traditional master, and Barrett, a Barrett not in revolt, wouldn't have dreamed of reproaching him for it. Losey doesn't seem to care about giving us other facts. He merely tells his story, describing in detail the slow decomposition of a master under the attack of his servant. But in all the rest of the film we have the explanation we want.

In any case, brutally, without any transition, Losey has us pass from the scene at the bar, where the valet begs forgiveness, to the living room of the house where the relationship between master and servant has been totally transformed. The valet growls at his master as a master normally would growl at his servant. He treats him as a lazy incompetent, which he is. He reproaches him for not bringing money home —this too is true; it is the role of the master to provide for the needs of the home. But he also complains of working too hard —"I do everything here; I'm killing myself with work"—which is absurd since, after all, this is the normal role of the servant. To sum up, the master is challenged on both levels; he doesn't fill the office of either master or valet; we no longer know just who he is, and just what this new, astonishing relationship between these two men consists of. There comes a crucial moment when Tony says: "I feel that we are two old comrades."

It is sentences like this that have led to the idea of a homosexual relationship between Tony and Barrett. Barrett would simply be jealous of the fiancée; it would thus be his confused feeling for Tony that makes him come back. And if Tony founders in this confusion, then takes back an insolent valet, it would be for the same reason. This is very possible; there is no work of art of any importance that doesn't allow several interpretations. However, it would be strange for Barrett, if sexually attracted by his master, to debase and then destroy him. And this interpretation would be not valid if one considers the other partner in the struggle: Susan. That would prove above all that everything can have a sexual meaning, and that human sexuality is almost always socialized. In any case, this sexual equality, from here on admitted by Tony and Barrett, makes the master disappear as master and the valet as valet. They are merely two young men, in a new relationship, which astonishes even them. I only offer as a proof—in this admirable and, I think, well-thought-out film—the following retort; Tony thinks and concludes: "The only time this happened to me was in the regiment." In other words, in a group of men, united in a fraternity that may well be virile, but also one in which social differences are abolished, confused in a relaxed anonymity. Isn't this exactly what Losey suggests: in a classless society, in which finally the master-servant relationship disappears? Where genuine human rapports could grow up between master and servant, if such rapports could last?

Of course, Losey and Pinter tell us at the same time that they can't last. The astounding game scene, between comrades, let loose across the apartment like two adolescents, confirms this unheard-of equality and its precariousness. After a badly thrown ball hits his eye, Barrett becomes angry; his master consoles him, begs him to calm down and then, to completely disarm him, suggests: "Let's say it's a draw, all right?"

Those words don't only sum up the game, they precisely place, as we shall see, the situation at this point of the film. We are even, at a pause. After this the master-servant relationship will completely reverse itself, this time in favor of the valet at the expense of the master. For a very brief moment the atmosphere is still fraternal, agreeably egalitarian. Then the valet, harshly, demands: "Now, go get me a cognac."

THE DOMESTIC SERVANT

III

Beginning at this point, it's all over: the inversion of the pendulum has started, and it will now go quickly. The master cooks and the servant doesn't find it to his taste; the servant demands respect, and the master must spare his feelings. The servant grumbles, and the master is afraid. The reversal is complete. We have already seen this in the colonies towards the end of colonization: as the colonizer begins to recoil under the offensive of the colonized, an unexpected moment arrives when he even begins to resemble the colonized; he begins to respect the colonized before being afraid, just as the colonized had been afraid for such a long time. This was really astounding for those who had lived in the colonies, who knew the overwhelming contempt in which the colonized live, so complete that it seemed legitimate for eternity. The fact is that the colonized had changed roles, before appearing as a deadly adversary. From then on, all is contested, all seems to change direction, everything is transformed into its opposite. Everything that was allowed to the master becomes the prerogative of the servant. All that was expected of the valet can now be asked of the master. Tony, who thought he would make use of the maid, is revealed as a toy in her hands; the erotic domination, normally due to the master, among other privileges, is no more than a degrading vice.

Let's once more take up the question: why such a radical transformation? Why such excess, such calculation, in the attack of the valet? Because he wanted to take his revenge on the fiancée, of course, and also of the master? But that's not enough to account for such a stubborn rage, such a premeditation of evil. To understand, there is no solution other than to come back again to the condition of the domestic,[1] in which there is probably this peculiarity: domestic alienation is one in which

---

[1] Dr. Le Guillant, whose book on *The Household Maid* is in preparation, uses the term, perhaps a better one, "servile condition."

the desire to identify with the master is at the same time the strongest and the most thwarted. One finds this wish on the part of the oppressed to identify with the oppressor everywhere: in the imitation of the colonizer by the colonized, in the masculinization of the woman. But it's all a matter of degree. Their lives are at this point so interwoven, by the very practice of the daily job, that they are in a way part of each other, so that it would be impossible for the servant to withdraw himself. Barrett prepares Tony's foot bath, takes his socks off, sees him in a daily sartorial sloppiness that is never shown to anyone else. When he uses his bed to make love to the maid-prostitute, and uses his eau de cologne and his shaving articles, he does so, of course, to penetrate his intimate life, but it is also true that he already shares this intimacy.

However, this forced identification is condemned, by definition, by the very agreement that brought it about, to remain about, to remain an illusion. There will never be a complete identification for there is a kind of denaturation of all the servant's acts, no matter how hard he applies himself, just as Christian sin will remain at the heart of all human behavior. The maid can wear her mistress's clothes, but the gift—still warm from the body of the benefactress—becomes, on the maid's body, an old garment, a symbol of her poverty. She wears a dress that her mistress has cast aside. The valet, dressed as his master dresses, even in new clothing, speaking the same language (borrowed from the dominant class), respecting the same values, occasionally even condemning those of his own people, will remain a caricature of his master.

This forever thwarted hope, this feeling of coming as close as possible and yet remaining infinitely far away, creates a state of unbearable tension. In the case of the Jew and the black man, self-hatred is often the result of an impossible self-rejection as much as that of the impossibility of identification. But in no case do we find such a painful conflict as in the relationship between servant and master, because of the day-to-day, haunting presence of the master. Dr. Le Guillant, who has studied this problem for many years and who has taken note of the frequency of this conflict in the household maid, has compared the relative figures of mental illness in this population group: they are, proportionally, frightening.

In this light we can better understand the astonishing furor that takes hold of domestic servants at times, the dreadful crimes of which they are capable: there seems to be no clue to an understanding of their behavior, no special interest, no banal resentment, not even sudden anger which transforms them into wild criminals, sadists, madmen, always unexpected. Barrett hounds Tony, beyond mere physical destruction, to the point of ridiculing him. He degrades him through drugs, he makes him walk on all fours, while onlookers jeer. It is the same paroxysm, the same absolute outburst that shocked all those who read of the case of the Papin sisters, those maids who so brutally disfigured the bodies of their mistresses to the point where they were no longer recognizable. This ugly exhibition of the excesses to which the revolt of the servant can lead was the subject of a French film, *Les Abysses*. Even Octave Mirabeau guessed at this many years ago.

"I ask Baptiste, the valet, jokingly: 'Well, Baptiste . . . and you? Your gift?'

" 'An oil drum, lighted under your bed.' "

It comes down to a matter of completely destroying the master. It can't be said that this violence is explained simply by the savagery or lack of culture of "those people," of a particularly beaten-down class. A young girl, a student who worked by chance as an *au pair* girl for an English family, told me of her unpleasant relationship with the mistress of the house, how she came to play all sorts of tricks to defend herself. "I used to turn the vacuum cleaner on, close the door and sit down to read. . . . It was agreed that I would eat at the table with them—the result was that I was serving them even during my meals. Then I decided I would eat in the kitchen, saying it was a matter of discretion on my part." One day she offered to fix her mistress's hair, saying that she had taken lessons in hairdressing when she had really never held a pair of scissors in her hand. Of course, she made her look hideous. "You should have seen her face afterwards, when she looked in the mirror, and the face of her husband. How upset they were!" she added with joy. This was a matter of an assault on her body, half realistic and half symbolic, actually closer to the realistic than to the symbolic. The young girl was making, vaguely, all the gestures of cutting off her mistress's head. While only a temporary domestic servant, she was still able to feel the bitterness of the situation and take stock of the weapons at her disposal.

Unfortunately, it seems that violence is inseparable from oppression, and therein lies the immense and unresolved problem. What horrifies us in the extraordinary violence of the domestic servant is that it seems unwarranted, unjustified. Materially at least, the life of the domestic is less miserable than that of other poor people, because of the domestic servant's direct dealings with the rich from whom he or she does gain advantages. When the domestic revolts, he does so in a frenzy, systematically destroying. The servant's attack against the master also seems scandalous. How can he or she take advantage of such a comfortable position? The master is too good to him; it's an abuse of confidence. Once again, there is a terrifying intuition on the part of Mirabeau: "When I think that each day a cook, for example, holds the life of his masters in his hands . . . a pinch of arsenic in place of salt . . . a drop of strychnine instead of vinegar . . . and that's that!"

Because of the ease with which it can be committed, the crime is too awful, as would be the crime that a doctor commits against his patient. But the doctor is not held in contempt, he is not scorned by his patients, he is not treated as a servant by those whose lives he holds in his hands. The inconsistency lies not only with the domestic, perhaps. There are certainly different conclusions to be drawn from these indications and many variations of them, but I am convinced that the key to the excessive violence of the domestic servant is found in this extremely intimate relationship between servant and master; because their lives are so interwoven in such an intimate manner, the servant will attack all the more angrily. The oppression of the domestic becomes more profound and more unbearable the more it is padded and in some ways accepted.

The life of the valet seems less miserable than that of the lives of other poor people. Materially, it certainly is: good lodgings, good food, good clothing. But there is another poverty, more serious perhaps, and that lies in the fact that he is the most *dependent* of all the poor; in one sense, the valet is perhaps the ideal poor man. He is the one who has most completely accepted his condition to the point where he seems to have reached an agreement with his master whereby the latter turns over to his care his very life, his body, his food, his children. The master says anything in front of the servant, shows him his true self apart from his behavior in society. But what an enormous price is paid for this confidence! He must exist as little as possible, must become his master's respectful shadow, listen to everything and pretend to have heard nothing, see everything without ever having seen anything. It is true that he is better dressed than other poor people, in that he imitates his master at his best; he wears a dignified suit while the worker is resigned to dirty and creased clothing, but the rich man never allows him to go beyond this imitation. This suit, clean and well cut, is recognizably different from that of the latter: *livery* is the costume of conceded dignity, that is to say agreed upon and denied by the same gesture. It is true that the servant has his master's ear every day, but do they talk *together*?[1] The use of the third person is a perfect symbol of the situation. In fact,

[1] When I address a maid as "Good day, Jeanine," this familiarity on my part is not only a kindness, since she cannot answer me using my first name. My greeting becomes the mark of the distance that separates us.

The Return of the Pendulum

the domestic doesn't have to talk at all (he merely answers his master when questioned), he acts when he is ordered to, he does not speak of himself, he is never anything but a reflection of his master. He has to give in to everything without being able to take comfort in language—the supreme human compensation, the best of outlets. The ideal image of the good servant, the big-hearted servant, the domestic faithful-until-death, contains an element of frankness and of a certain grumbling. It must be true that the best master-servant relationships are those in which the servant can compensate for his humiliation by means of some slightly comforting verbal revenge.

This is why, in the end, the servant, far from being envied, is most often held in contempt and made fun of by other poor people. They are not wrong; they paid a great deal for their few advantages. All the poor work for the rich, but most often indirectly, and when they work directly for the rich they are tied only by their tasks. The domestic servant is in his master's service for every part of his life. The contempt the poor people have for the domestics has nothing to do with the quality of the work done, but it is based on the meaning of the work, on the servant's complete debasement, a debasement to which he consents. Naturally, this contempt the poor feels towards the domestic, that the domestic feels for himself, is a reflection of the general contempt in which the poor are held by the rich to which the poor always to some extent resign themselves. But in this case it is a special contempt for those who have surrendered, who have accepted domination to the point where it becomes part of their lives. The valet is, finally, a traitor to the common condition of the poor. That is why he is so often accused and repulsed by the other oppressed peoples, and, through an obvious contradiction, suspected by the masters.

From time to time this explodes in an insane act, literally insane. But I don't believe that insane acts are without some explanation. Violence is not an abnormal reaction, it is a total reaction to a situation which has reached its limit. The domes-

THE DOMESTIC SERVANT

tic servant who takes his revenge becomes in effect a madman
who destroys everything, and destroys himself. He doesn't even
hide, he allows himself to be taken by the police rather easily,
he acknowledges his crime in poisoning his master's food. We
ask why such violence against others and against themselves,
why the vengeance is such a terrible one. We have seen this in
the case of the black Americans: the spring which has been
held back so long is abruptly released, it runs against the path
of the injustice with an increased violence: the return of the
pendulum seems to be a phenomenon common to all violence.

One final question concerning this admirable, meaningful
film: Is this violence, this reverse shock, an adequate solution
to the humiliation of the domestic servant? Here is Losey's final
comment. At the end of the orgy scene, in which Tony has
submitted to every possible insult, even being symbolically
cuckolded by Barrett, the wretched man slams his foot on the
table and cries out: "That's enough!" What does Barrett do
then? Obediently, and this obedience does not seem at all false,
the valet says: "All right . . . Everybody out. . . . Clear out,"
and he sends all the prostitutes out to the street. The master has
been obeyed, he remains once and for all the master.

Pretense? Temporary obedience? Will the destruction continue the next day? Maybe, but if it is a ruse, it is because
something must be considered—the respect due to the master,
in spite of everything. At the door, Susan slaps Barrett, hard,
after having returned to him his heavy metal bracelet. Not only
doesn't Barrett revolt and return the blow, but he lowers his
head, leans his forehead against the door for a moment and
then helps the young woman on with her coat, once again playing the role of the valet. He probably feels somewhat guilty as
well. But at the point at which the three partners find themselves, he could have spared himself this servile gesture. In doing it, he once again defines for himself his function and his
rank. Each person takes up his position again. Everything happens as if, in spite of these terrifying excesses, there is nonethe-

The Return of the Pendulum

less a limit: the master remains master and the valet remains valet.

Actually, for this distribution of social roles to end, it would have been necessary to put a complete end to the servant-master relationship, to alter totally the bond beween Tony and Barrett. Otherwise there will be a series of steps towards mutual destruction. There we can begin to understand the temptation of physical violence which would lead to the final destruction of this relationship. So what if the murder of the master turns out to be suicide as well. It is also clear, however, that murder and suicide are not *solutions* to this relationship, since they don't really transform it. The fury of the Papin sisters, the shocking dreams of Mirabeau's characters and Barrett's sadism do not really break the figure of the master. (This can explain the brutal attack, a desperate one both real and symbolic, on the eyes and face of the victims; the endless exasperation, never being satisfied.) The only true solution, violent or not, would obviously be for the servant to stop existing and acting in relationship to his master. The return of the pendulum, understandable as it may be, is still no more than an inverted submission. This has been illustrated in the case of the colonized. For the oppressed to be finally free, he must go beyond revolt, by another path, he must begin in other ways, conceive of himself and reconstruct himself independently of his master.

(*Translated by Howard Greenfeld*)

RACISM
AND
OPPRESSION

(First published in *NEF,* a special number on racism, Paris, 1964.)

14

Attempt at a Definition

Of course the definition which follows is the result of all the following commentary and analysis. I am beginning with it for memory's sake, in an expository procedure like that used by mathematicians. These pages could just as well be read in reverse order: sections III, II, and I. The best way would be to run rapidly through the definition and the analysis even if it is necessary to come back to them in the light of the commentary.

I. *Definition*

Racism is the generalized and final assigning of values to real or imaginary differences, to the accuser's benefit and at his victim's expense, in order to justify the former's own privileges or aggression.

RACISM AND OPPRESSION

II. Analysis of the Racist Attitude

This analysis reveals four essential elements:

1) Stressing the *real or imaginary differences* between the racist and his victim.

2) *Assigning values* to these differences, to the advantage of the racist and the detriment of his victim.

3) Trying to make them *absolutes* by *generalizing* from them and claiming that they are final.

4) *Justifying* any present or possible *aggression* or *privilege*.[1]

III. Commentary

The term "racism" is obviously not adequate to cover a mechanism so widespread. It is too narrow, just as "anti-Semitism" is, on the contrary, too broad. Strictly speaking, it would apply to a theory of biological differences. The Nazis, adding to the ideas of the apologists for the slave trade and for colonization, included a system for establishing a political, moral and cultural hierarchy of human groups according to their biological differences.

A WIDESPREAD MECHANISM

The racist actually bases his accusation on a biological or a cultural difference, from which he generalizes to cover the whole of the defendant's personality, his life and the group to which he belongs. Sometimes the biological trait is unclear or even missing. We can see that the mechanism is infinitely more varied, more complex and—unhappily—more common than the term "racism" would imply. It ought to be replaced by another term or other words showing what varied and at the same time what interrelated forms racism can take.[2]

---

[1] If further summary were necessary, I would say that racism seems to me to include three essential elements: insisting on a *difference;* putting it to *mythical use;* the *convenience* of such use.

[2] Perhaps by a pair of terms: "aggression-justification," for instance,

STRESSING THE DIFFERENCE

The first form of racism consists of stressing a *difference* between the accuser and his victim. But revealing a characteristic differentiating two individuals or two groups does not in itself constitute a racist attitude. After all, this is part of what any student of the human sciences does. The assertion that there is a difference takes on a special *significance* in the racist context: by emphasizing the difference, the racist aims to intensify or cause the *exclusion*, the *separation* by which the victim is placed outside the community or even outside humanity.

The colonizer discriminates to demonstrate the impossibility of including the colonized in the community: because he would be too biologically or culturally different, technically or politically inept, etc. Anti-Semitism attempts, by depicting the Jew as radically foreign and strange, to explain the isolation of the Jew, the quarantine under which he is placed. Making use of the difference is an essential step in the racist process: *but it is not the difference which always entails racism; it is racism which makes use of the difference.*

THE DIFFERENCE IS REAL OR IMAGINARY

If the difference is missing, the racist invents one; if the difference exists, he interprets it to his own advantage. He emphasizes only those differences which contribute to his argument. In other words, the difference is real or imaginary, important or slight in itself.

One important point, however: contrary to the view commonly held by the sentimental anti-racist, I do not think that the difference singled out by the racist is always the work of imagination, sheer madness or a malevolent lie. The racist can base his argument on a *real trait*, whether biological, psycho-

---

which sums up quite well the general mechanism we are about to describe.

logical, cultural or social—such as the color of the black man's skin or the solid tradition of the Jew.[1]

Of course the racist can make up a difference, if he needs one to construct his argument, but his method is not confined to imagining more or less fantastic differential traits nor to the mere observation of sometimes genuine differences. It always adds an *interpretation* of such differences, a prejudiced attempt to *place a value* on them.[2] To put it briefly, the difference is assigned a value in such a way as to discredit the defendant and reflect credit on his accuser.

PLACING A VALUE ON THE DIFFERENCE

Here is certainly one of the key elements in the racist process. Explicitly or implicitly, the assigning of values is intended to prove two things: the inferiority of the victim *and* the superiority of the racist. Better still, it proves the one by the other: inferiority of the black race automatically means superiority of the white. Inferiority of the colonized vividly demonstrates the superiority of the colonizer. Thus, the assigning of values is negative and positive at the same time: negative value of the victim, therefore positive value of the accuser. It follows that:

1) any difference separating the victim from his accuser is likely to be suspect and deserve denunciation. Racism begins by assigning a negative value and, simply by changing a minus to a plus sign, can turn any difference, whether real or imagined, into a positive quality on the part of the accuser. In the racist way of thinking, *difference is evil.* This means, of course,

[1] Or even at times a genuine *inadequacy.* Of course, the racist, far from viewing it as a result of the oppression to which he himself subjects his victim or at least of the objective conditions which the victim is made to endure, holds that inadequacy against him, as if it were a defect or flaw. Examples: the technical unpreparedness of the colonized, which is the result of colonization; or the high rate of absenteeism among working women, the result of their family duties.

[2] I have run into a good deal of argument over this phrase, *"placing a value on the difference."* Here of course it has the strict meaning of assigning either a *negative* or a *positive* value.

the difference characterizing the victim in relation to the accuser, who is taken as the point of reference. It is not whiteness that differentiates the white man from the black; it is blackness that disastrously differentiates the black man from the white.

2) the racist will do his utmost to stretch the distance between the minus and the plus signs, to *maximize the difference*. The smaller he makes his victim, the bigger he becomes; the more drastically he marks the difference at the expense of his victim, the more drastically he turns it to his own advantage.[1]

That is why a simple biological or cultural difference, which is sometimes a real one, brings a whole crowd of meanings in its wake: the biology of the Jew becomes a repulsive biology, an unhealthful one. One step further, and it becomes heavy with a specific, harmful psychology, then with a metaphysical life of its own, etc. . . . We go from biology to ethics, from ethics to politics, from politics to metaphysics.

Once a value has been assigned, the coherence of the consequences emerges, and it is apparent that the noxious and inflamatory difference, overwhelming the victim and flattering his accuser, must be made *absolute*. If the accuser wants to be radically superior, then the difference must be made radical.

THE DIFFERENCE IS GENERALIZED

So the discriminatory process enters the stage of generalization, "totalization." One thing leads to another until *all of the victim's personality* is characterized by the difference, and *all of the members* of his social group are targets for the accusation.

1) In this perspective it is easier to understand why biological racism is so successful; it fits in particularly well. The disastrous difference is echoed, as it were, in a substratum: it penetrates the flesh, the blood and the genes of the victim. It is transformed into fate, destiny, heredity. From then on, the vic-

---

[1] See, in *The Colonizer and the Colonized* the notion of the "*Negro complex*," which also includes this see-saw movement, both complementary and contradictory.

tim's very *being* is contaminated, and likewise *every manifestation of that being*: behavior, body and soul. Rarely does biological racism fail to give rise to psychological and cultural racism. In fact, the whole might be called an *ethnism*.

2) If the difference penetrates so profoundly into the being of the victim, it must also penetrate *all his family*, who are part of the same being.[1]

This is not actually a generalization: the relation between the individual trait and the collective trait is, so to speak, dialectic. Each of the defendant's real or supposed defects is extended to all his equals, but it is in the name of an implied collective defect that the defendant is condemned. From the greed of one Jew the anti-Semite concludes that all Jews are greedy and decides that no single Jew can be trusted because all Jews are greedy. The same is true with the stereotype of the lazy colonized.

Racism, on whatever level it occurs, always includes this *collective* element which is, of course, one of the best ways of totalizing the situation: there must be no loophole by which any Jew, any colonized or any black man could escape this *social determinism*.

THE DIFFERENCE IS FINAL

It is easy to understand how the same movement also extends through *time*, back into the past and forward into the future. The Jew has always been greedy, the black man has always been inferior. Conclusion: the Jew will always be greedy, the black man will always be inferior; there is no hope of a change, no salvation to be expected. *Globalization, totalization, social generalization* and *temporal generalization*—all tend to a single purpose which, in the extreme, would be a substantiation of the difference, than of the victim as a figure. Thus, there is said to be a sort of absolute black man, a kind of absolute Jew. They are negative figures, of course; definitively and absolutely nega-

---

[1] See, ibid., *"the mark of the plural."*

tive. In the Middle Ages, as we know, the Jew finally became one of the incarnations of the devil, and in our own country he became the radical and antithetical enemy of the Nazis. In the same way the black man has become one of the inferior categories of the human species. *In the extreme, racism merges into myth.*

At this point the whole structure takes leave of reality, from which it had derived its strength for a time, and follows its own coherence, moving from mere accusation to myth through the successive stages by which the victim is stripped of value. Broadly speaking, the process is one of *gradual dehumanization.* The racist ascribes to his victim a series of surprising traits, calling him incomprehensible, impenetrable, mysterious, strange, disturbing, etc. Slowly he makes of his victim a sort of animal, a thing or simply a symbol.

As the outcome of this effort to expel him from any human community, the victim is chained once and for all to his destiny of misfortune, derision and guilt. And as a counterpart, the accuser is assured once and for all of keeping his role as rightful judge.

JUSTIFICATION OF THE ACCUSER

While racism moves toward myth, *the myth refers back to the racist.*

It is in the racist himself that the motives for racism lie. A superficial analysis is enough to reveal them, whether in individual or collective aggression.

I will not repeat the now classic analyses of two phenomena: the scapegoat, and the foreigner corrupting the national soul. We are already familiar with the way a group of human beings, in order to rid itself of certain guilt feelings, projects them onto an object, an animal, a man or another group, which it accuses and punishes in its own stead. Nor will I linger over the alibi type of racism, an excuse for individual aggression. Competition on the economic front, rivalry between intellectuals or art-

RACISM AND OPPRESSION

ists—these can give rise to racism, as a way of justifying *a priori* every difficulty the accuser runs into and his behavior toward his adversary. There is even a less sordid, distinctly *individual motivation*[1] which has been largely overlooked so far. A certain embarrassment when faced with what is different, the anxiety which results, spontaneous recourse to aggression in order to push back that anxiety—all of these are to be found in children, and probably in a good many adults as well. Whatever is different or foreign can be felt as a disturbing factor, hence a source of scandal. The attempt to wipe it out follows naturally. This is a primitive, virtually animal reaction, but it certainly goes deeper than we care to admit. We will have to give it more serious study instead of trying to sidestep it by optimistic moralizing. However that may be, the mechanism remains the same. By an accurate or a falsified characterization of the victim, the accuser attempts to explain and to *justify* his attitude and his behavior toward him.

JUSTIFYING INJUSTICE

But what sort of attitude and behavior are these, that they need to be justified? Why does the accuser feel obliged to accuse in order to justify himself? *Because he feels guilty toward his victim.* Because he feels that his attitude and his behavior are essentially unjust and fraudulent. Here, in fact, we must turn the racist's argument inside out: he does not punish his victim because his victim deserves to be punished; he calls him

---

[1] Yet the fact of an individual motivation does not cancel out the mediation of the social factor, which I consider crucial in any racist process. Individual motivation does not become genuine racism until it is filtered through the culture and the ideologies of a group. In the prevailing stereotypes it seeks, and finds, the explanation of its own uneasiness, which is then turned into racism. The individual racist actually discovers discrimination all about him—in his education and his culture—as a potential mental attitude, and he adopts it when he feels the need to do so. The intermediary of society is felt on two levels: that of the victim, as member of a guilty and defective group, and that of the accuser, representative of a normal and healthy group.

guilty because he is *already* punished or, at best, because he, the accuser, is preparing to punish him.

Proof? *In almost every case, the punishment has already been inflicted.* The victim of racism is *already* living under the weight of disgrace and oppression. The racist does not aim his accusations at the mighty but at the vanquished. The Jew is already ostracized, the colonized is already colonized. In order to justify such punishment and misfortune, a process of rationalization is set in motion, by which to explain away the ghetto and the colonial exploitation.

Very often, the precarious nature of the victim's life, the injustice of it are independent of the will of any individual. *Racism is the objective counterpart of the victim's objective situation.* Examples: women suffer because they have deserved to suffer; the black man is a slave because he has been cast out. The individual can be tempted by this collective reasoning; it forms part of the values held by his peers and relieves him of the weight of any responsibility. Where everyone tolerates and condones scandal, scandal disappears.

RACISM AND OPPRESSION

This is why racism accompanies almost every kind of oppression: *racism is one of the best justifications of and symbols for oppression.* I have found it in the colonial relationship, in anti-Semitism and in oppression of the black man. More or less explicitly, it is also found in the condition of the proletarian worker, the servant, and so on.

Of course it varies subtly, emerging differently from one social and historical context to another, from one form of oppression to another. The common denominator must not obscure the need, in each case, to look for the distinguishing features of each context: quite the contrary. As I have amply shown, the racist accusation, although it follows a relatively monotonous and banal pattern, should suggest something else: the precise context, the specific oppression which is the real cause of the

RACISM AND OPPRESSION

racist alibi. The black man is labeled congenitally good-for-nothing so that he can be kept in economic bondage; the colonized is tagged as unfit to handle anything technical so that colonization can last; the proletarian as politically and socially childish so that the domination of the property-owning classes can continue unchallenged. To come to the end of each particular form of racism, we will have to tackle colonization or the social and political structure of our societies.

The fact remains that *we have discovered a fundamental mechanism,* common to all racist reactions: the *injustice of an oppressor toward the oppressed,* the former's permanent *aggression* or the aggressive act he is getting ready to commit, *must be justified.* And isn't privilege one of the forms of permanent aggression, inflicted on a dominated man or group by a dominating man or group? How can any excuse be found for such disorder (source of so many advantages) if not by overwhelming the victim? Underneath its masks, *racism is the racist's way of giving himself absolution.*

THE DEFINITION ONCE AGAIN

Now we can come back to the definition offered in the beginning to summarize the essential points of this commentary:

Racism is the generalized and final assigning of values to real or imaginary differences, to the accuser's benefit and at his victim's expense, in order to justify the former's own privileges or aggression.

Memo on Fighting and Treating Racism

On the basis of the definition and the commentary relating to it, can we deduce a technique for taking action against racism?

I have been forced, as we have seen, to abandon once and for all that *sociology of good intentions,* or psycho-pathology, which looks on racism as a monstrous and incomprehensible aberration on the part of certain social groups or a sort of madness on the part of certain individuals. (The Nazi movement, for instance, is called an "inexplicable" phenomenon in twentieth century Europe, and the racist's behavior is written off as vaguely pathological.) Whereas in fact there are *bases* for racism within the individual human being and within the social group. Racism is made operative by *mechanisms* which have their own special coherence. Any fight against racism must start with knowledge of these bases and these mechanisms and must act upon them.

In other words, it is an *information* campaign that is called for, as well as a genuinely *political* fight.

The information and education campaign involves rethinking the notion of *difference*. For the racist, whether out of embarrassment or out of fear of the unknown, difference is bad and should be punished. It is paradoxical that neither the humanist nor the anti-racist contradicts this; both are content to deny that the difference exists—which is a way of dodging the issue. We must come around to recognizing certain differences among human beings and to showing that these differences are neither harmful nor scandalous.[1]

The political fight must be planned around a separate analysis of each context. Who benefits from the arguments justifying racism? What privilege or act of aggression does it prepare for or conceal? Then, if we really want to get at racism, we must tackle this concrete relationship, *this implicit or explicit oppression*.

Otherwise we will go on doing nothing more than expressing the indignation proper to sentimental anti-racism, which achieves as little as it costs.

(Translated by Eleanor Levieux)

[1] See the conclusions reached in *The Colonizer and the Colonized* and *Portrait of a Jew*. The colonized should not, any more than the Jew or the black, be unfaithful to himself or use camouflage in order to disarm his prejudiced adversaries. He should insist on being accepted as he is, differences and all.

(Written as the basis of the conclusion to *Les Français et le racism* by A. Memmi, P. H. Maucorps and J. F. Held, Editions Payot, Paris, 1965.)

15

Racism and Oppression

Everyone seems to be against racism. At least no one says openly that he himself is a racist. Even those who practice discrimination, in both words and actions, do not defend it as a philosophy. They are almost unanimous in explaining those words and those actions in a way which, they insist, has nothing to do with racism.

Of course we could accept this at face value. Or we could try to understand the phenomenon of racism, even if comprehension is likely to prove more disturbing than general indignation, in the long run. In this approach racism is taken as a topic for study; for the time being any moral issues must be left aside, and so, to some extent, must any concern with taking action.

Having chosen the second approach, we have discovered a certain number of characteristics of racism; they seem fairly decisive and, as we suspected, not so reassuring:

1) *Everyone, or nearly everyone, is an unconscious racist,* or a semi-conscious one, or even a conscious one. The degrees range from the man who starts out, "I don't have any prejudice against any race, but . . ." to the one who claims the black

man has a peculiar smell or the Jew a "concentration camp" look. From the man who professes to be anti-racist and yet cannot help feeling uncomfortably hesitant, to the defiant attitude of the nearly-avowed racist, who embraces everything about racism except the label. From the European who criticizes segregation in America but would avoid renting a room to a black student, to the Frenchman who upholds the methods of the Ku Klux Klan and would apply them in his own country if he could. All of these people offer ways to interpret and rationalize the attitudes they take and the speeches they make, but all of them, in the last analysis, share a *common denominator.* The man who speaks up for the Ku Klux Klan asserts that the hooded Americans want to defend their country, the virtue of their women and the color of their children's skin. Similarly, the man who merely refuses to rent a room to a black man and admits that he feels uneasy—even if he admits that he shouldn't—at seeing a black man walking with a white woman is also thinking, in a confused way, of the purity of women and the color of his country's children yet unborn.

While from one to the other the interpretation differs, becoming an explanation, a travesty, or an alibi, it always refers back to the same fact. It may be more or less out in the open, or more or less disguised, but it is always discernible.

2) In short, *racism is one of the most widespread attitudes in the world.* Racial prejudice is a *social fact.* This in itself is enough to explain why it is so important, so varied, so extensive, so deep and so general. This also means that it pre-exists, imposing itself on the individual.

In still other words, before taking root in the individual, racism has taken root in the institutions and ideologies all around him, in the education he receives and the culture he acquires.

It would be interesting to film one of these cultural circuits: the way the ideologists create ideologies from relations between forces and institutions; the way journalists vulgarize those ideologies and the newspaper reader swallows their diluted

RACISM AND OPPRESSION

poison in such repeated doses that it soaks into him completely. Never has it been adequately pointed out that writers and literature of even the highest sort play an insidious role in propagating racist themes and images.[1] Religions themselves are not sinless in this respect. And lastly, the family circle is an extraordinary *culture medium* for prejudices, fears and resentments from which few children emerge wholly uncontaminated. First and foremost, racism is as intimate a part of the child's familial and social upbringing as the milk he sucks in infancy.

3) Why is this? Why is an attitude so negative and so obviously detrimental to the communal life of men so universal?

We promised that we would try to understand, instead of trying to reassure ourselves at all costs or merely waxing indignant over some people's unexpected wickedness. The truth is that the *racist explanation is convenient.* That is why it is so easily and so commonly used both by individuals and by the group: it is too tempting to be resisted.

Because it corresponds somehow to what is evident and is somehow confirmed, the racist accusation is a widespread and persuasive social fact. *It is a psycho-social fact, because racism is an institutional fact.*

The colonized was not only accused of being a second-class man. *He was in fact just that:* he did not have the same rights as the colonizer himself. The black American is not only described as a misfit: far too often he *is just that.* The Jew *is* genuinely separate and is placed under a more or less discreet form of quarantine.

Since it is a matter for observation that the *object of racism* is inferior and is ground down, isn't it tempting to look on the *racist ideology as an adequate expression of that objective situation?* To say that if the Jew is separate, it is probably because something in him naturally alienates others and deserves to be kept separate? To explain that if the fate of the colonized is so

[1] See *Portrait of a Jew,* chapter 6, part I.

overwhelming and so miserable, it is because he was ripe to become the target of colonialism?

Of course one could stand up and say the situation is the other way around: it is the ideology, the accusation inflated to mythical proportions which explains and legitimatizes the iniquitous situation of the *person discriminated against*. But whoever spoke out so boldly would immediately have to blame himself, his family and his entire universe for having made the victim such a *victim*—and who would have strength enough to do that? It would take lucidity, honesty and courage such as even so-called highly cultured men are scarcely capable of. It is more "natural," more spontaneous, and so much more *convenient* to look for an explanation which soothes the deep-lying guilt felt by both individual and group toward the *victim of racism*.

4) The racist explanation is, after all, the most *effective*. "Euphoria-inducing," as the psychologists put it, it is a great help to the anxious and avid Narcissus concealed in each one of us. It reassures and flatters the racist, excuses and strengthens him by reinforcing his individual and collective ego.

And so economically too! By making the other people pay! The racist finds joy, solace and vindication at the expense of others. He doesn't even have to boast; he merely belittles the others to set off his own qualities. His superiority does not have to be proven, since it is implied in the other man's inferiority.

The racist temptation is certainly the one least resisted—such an inexpensive vice, that does not even appear to be bad for the sinner's health, since it is practiced to *other* people's detriment. Why not give in to a craving so easy to satisfy and so common, for that matter?

5) *To be big, all the racist need do is climb on someone else's back.*

It is easy to understand why he chooses for this purpose the most obvious and resigned of victims, the one who submits to

RACISM AND OPPRESSION

blows in silence, the victim who is already the most victimized: the most convenient step in the whole very convenient process.

You never hear of anti-American or anti-British, or even anti-German racism: these are men who are historically strong, backed up by powerful nations. Whereas the racist wrings his triumph only out of men whom history has already defeated, the weaker links in the chain of humanity. *The racist instinctively chooses the oppressed,* heaping more misfortune on the unfortunate.

6) For this reason the foreigner is choice prey for the racist, a promising and unhoped-for rung on which the posturing victor can place his foot to climb higher. *Which explains the obvious, intimate relationship between racism and xenophobia.* The vulnerability of the foreigner arouses racism, just as infirmity arouses sarcasm and scorn.

7) This accounts for the surprising *racism practiced by the oppressed man himself.* Sure enough, the proletarian, the colonized, the Negro, the black man—all can turn around and be racists too. How can one victim attack another? Simply enough: by the same process and in response to the same temptation. If the French proletarian wants to feel a little taller, whom is he to step on if not on the immigrant worker, who has been North African so far but might also be Italian, Spanish or Polish—in other words, of the same so-called race as himself? Proof, if proof were needed, that racism is not always directly connected with race. If the modest colonizer, himself so taken advantage of and so disinherited, wanted to take revenge, what other target was there than the colonized, whom he could look down upon from the limited height of those meager privileges which the colonial system gave him? So it is that the American Jew may be tempted to scorn the American black, who reciprocates heartily.

Everyone looks for an inferior rank compared to which he appears relatively lofty and grand. Racism offers everyone the solution that suits him best; he need only find someone smaller,

Racism and Oppression

more humiliated than himself, and there he has his victim, the target for his scorn and prejudice. *Racism is a pleasure within everyone's reach.*

8) But do men really have such a terrible urge to reassure and reassert themselves, even at the cost of humiliating others, to justify themselves even by accusing others? Once we realize how extensive this compulsion is, how often this solution is adopted, then we are forced to realize that the answer is yes.

Certainly the solution is false, the compensation vain, small and above all unjust, distorting criteria and warping perspectives, self-deceiving, destroying one man's dignity to give another the illusion of dignity. But it must be admitted that it *is a sort of a solution to genuine problems,* a tranquilizer for disturbances so manifest and so common that we would be surprised if we did not find them.

The sick man consoles himself with the thought that others are even more sick than he; he has a vague idea that there are still several degrees between himself and death and that, compared to so-and-so, he is not so badly off after all. It is a fact that misery consoles misery. Is it surprising then that the racist takes a rest from his own misery by looking at the next man's? He even goes one step further, claiming that the next man is more miserable, unfortunate and perverse than he really is.

This is made all the easier by the fact that the next man is virtually never neutral. Not enough emphasis has been placed on a particular ingredient of racism, which is the uneasiness and *fear aroused by differentness.* The foreigner, or even merely a man of another social class, is always somewhat strange and frightening. It is only a few short steps from fear to hostility, and from hostility to aggression. Loving means relaxing, yielding, forgetting oneself in the other person, identifying with him more or less. You do not forgive a foreigner until you have managed to adopt him. Otherwise he continues to be inscrutable, to resist, as it were, and your reaction is one of anxiety and irritation. How can you help resenting people who force you to

RACISM AND OPPRESSION

remain on the defensive? And now affective logic, that misnamed upside-down reasoning, comes into play: how can these people you suspect and sentence beforehand help but turn around and resent you?

9) From this point on, the passions whirl around in a vicious circle of "reasoning" like this: since these people probably detest us, they certainly deserve to have us hate them, and mustn't we take precautions against their possible acts of aggression by acting aggressively against them if necessary, etc., etc. . . . ? Any number of battles, both individual and collective, grow chiefly out of such mean and devious arguments, designed to exorcise fear of the next man and soothe a troubled conscience.

Guilt feelings constitute one of the most powerful driving forces in the racist mechanism. Why do privilege and oppression arouse such a strong racist reaction? Because racism is undoubtedly one way of combating that inner misery which is remorse. If there is oppression it must be because someone is guilty, and if the oppressor himself does not plead guilty—a situation which would soon become intolerable—then it must be the oppressed man who is guilty. *In short, by means of racism, the victim is blamed for the real or imaginary crimes of the racist.*

10) In that case, what can be done? What indeed, if the evil is so deeply rooted and so widespread, so much a part of our institutions and our collective thoughts, so tempting and seemingly so inexpensive? But I don't believe it really is inexpensive; I maintain that like any other oppression, racism deforms the racist himself, both his appearance and his behavior, just as imperialism transformed even Europeans of good will into imperialists. But here again, tremendous lucidity would be required to realize the harm done to oneself by fear, authority and privileges. What can actually be done to wipe out the creeping infection?

It seems that we must *bring our sympathy into action,*[1] that we must make the painstaking effort *to put ourselves in the other man's place.* This sort of wisdom is as old as time; it is the best way of understanding how someone else suffers, how insults and blows humiliate and pain him. Through our thoughts, at least, we achieve a kind of empathy. The ultimate effort is to try to live certain situations ourselves—to live in the black man's skin, as in the astounding experiment carried out by the white American, Griffith, or actually to share the daily existence of the working man, as certain political militants or the worker-priests compel themselves to do. There can be no doubt, in such a case, that when led by the body and the mind, the imagination, usually so lazy where others are concerned, is made to participate. No doubt either that this is the most effective form of mental hygiene to prevent racism from setting in.

11) But precisely because this process is so noble and demands so much of the individual, it should be completed by more *collective measures. Education* will certainly continue to be the best technique for training and liberating mankind. Because it is a slow process, and a preventive one, because it reaches out to the young, because it acts continuously on the individual and at the same time influences great masses, education (which should be accompanied by a campaign for *adult enlightenment*) must always aim to discover what needs to be done so that men will cease to carry arms against one another and their natural aggressiveness can be put to a different use.

12) But the main point, I think, is this. *The fight against racism coincides, at least partly, with the fight against oppression.* For fight there will be, necessarily. Racism is not only a perverted feeling; it is also the result, the expression, and the adjunct of a *de facto* situation which must be changed if racism

[1] Or we must "empathize," to borrow the precise expression of my friend and colleague, the French sociologist, P. H. Maucorps.

RACISM AND OPPRESSION

is to be defeated. This means that the *oppressed man must cease to be oppressed,* to be the easily victimized embodiment of the oppressor's guilt feelings. The counterpart is that *the oppressor must stop being an oppressor,* stop having a convenient victim, needing to have one and needing to find an excuse for that need.

Of course the idea is not to strip man entirely of his aggressiveness, as some racists sarcastically claim it is. They hide behind a poor excuse for philosophy, allegedly virile but actually based on disdain for the human being and his possible destruction. A man needs a certain amount of aggressiveness. It would be unhealthful and even dangerous if a man were never able to hate and even, on occasion, to strike.

But his quasi-normal hesitation in the face of differentness must not become the instrument and the alibi for his injustice. Prejudice must not turn into myth. He must not feel entitled to bully any individual because that person belongs to a group covered by a blanket accusation of depravity.

Many anti-racists, swept away by an oversimplifying generosity, maintain that every real difference between men must be denied. But this is not necessary. On the contrary, *the differences must be luckily acknowledged,* admitted and respected as such. Once the other man is recognized as another man, such differences can even become a source of self-enrichment, as recognition encourages dialogue and brings it about. Whereas denying the differences, closing one's eyes to an undeniable aspect of human reality is liable to result in dangerous astonishment and a spectacular about-face the day those differences are finally brought home to even the most generous of humanists: a painful experience to which many of them, and many teachers in the colonies, can already testify.[1]

---

[1] I take this opportunity to clarify a point concerning humanism: in recent decades, humanism has been the object of a great many attacks, and I myself have mocked the humanists. But a distinction must be made among different sorts of attack. The fascists too violently con-

When face to face with differentness, and the problems it inevitably creates, there are two possible reactions: war, or dialogue. The temptation to defeat someone else, reduce him to servitude, and find some ideological pretext for doing so is certainly very common, and seems more worthwhile than beginning a dialogue and deciding on measures of equitable reciprocity.

13) Here is where an ethical and political *option* comes into play. Until now we have deliberately left it aside. A choice must be made between an attitude and a type of behavior which crush and humiliate certain men in order to exalt others, and an attitude and behavior which originate in the belief that all men are of equal dignity. Here is the dividing line between racists and anti-racists. The racist accepts this type of primitive violence and claims to justify it; the end result is undeniably a certain philosophy of man and of human relationships. The anti-racist rejects such a rupture between men and refuses to place them in two categories from which there is no appeal: the inferior and the superior. He believes dialogue is possible and is willing to reconsider existing situations and privileges. *In the last analysis, the dividing line runs between two views of man and two philosophies.*

14) One final word: *there is no denying the difficulty of the fight against racism.*

It is not easy to put oneself in the place of the oppressed

---

demned the humanists and sneered at them, because the humanists fought against the image of man which the fascists had drawn.

Our own impatience had a different meaning, of course. We simply regretted that the humanists were so carried away by their generous impulse towards universal man, towards brotherhood based on reason and on a denominator common to all men that they neglected the concrete, specific problems of such and such individual man. Not to mention that the man involved was often a man in a difficult historical situation, such as the colonized or the Jew. A serious oversight, since humanism was in danger of becoming the philosophy of an alibi.

This is not to say, by any means, that I deny the humanist ideal. It should be furthered. It leads the way.

RACISM AND OPPRESSION

man, whoever he may be; the difficulty of "taking part" in someone else becomes greater as the oppressed man becomes more oppressed, i.e., as the social and psychological *distance* between himself and other men increases. Often the gap between the colonized and even the best-intentioned colonizer was so wide that the white European had no notion of what was going on within the soul of his "impenetrable" native servant. Moreover, the victim of oppression feels that there is no way out; no man who is not oppressed has experienced despair and anguish to this degree. The non-oppressed man who tries to put himself in the victim's place can, by definition, call a halt to his experiment. No matter how sincere Griffith, the white American, was in dyeing his skin and living as a black among blacks in the South, he knew that whenever he wanted to he could go back up North, announce "I'm white," and bring his voluntary nightmare to an end. No one can ever put himself completely in the place of a black man nor in that of a Jew whose family has been exterminated in a crematory.

At the same time, what is taught in the schools must overcome what is taught in the home and the street. It will have to uproot the entire cultural tradition which, being vague and incoherent, offers that much more resistance.

Only by transforming the objective conditions of existence can an end be put to the various forms of oppression, and this transformation will not happen overnight. It does not depend on the strength of the anti-racists alone. Nor is there any guarantee that once a much-fought-for political order has been established, it will not, during some social crisis, turn around and use the time-tested racist alibi itself.

The struggle to combat racism is long and arduous, an attack to be launched again and again, a campaign that will probably never be ended.

Yet for that very reason it is a fight which should be fought without respite and without concession. We cannot be indulgent towards racism any more than we would deliberately bring a monster into our house even—still less—if the monster were disguised. Doing that would mean giving it a chance, putting the animal and the humane sides of ourselves and other men into the scales, and finding that they came down on the side of the animal. What would it mean to accept the racist's way of thinking, even just slightly? It would mean endorsing fear, injustice and violence. Agreeing that no light is to pierce the dimness and obscurity in which we are still largely accustomed to living. Agreeing that the foreigner is to remain a potential victim. (But what man is not a foreigner—to someone else?) In short, racism illustrates the totally negative condition of subjugated man and in a certain way sheds light on the entire human condition. While the fight against racism is demanding and its outcome always uncertain, it is one of the indispensable preliminaries to the progress from animality to humanity. *We cannot afford not to take up the racist challenge.*

(*Translated by Eleanor Levieux*)

Postscript

At the time I was reading the proofs of this book, the student crisis and its repercussions broke out throughout the entire world. Beyond its specific meaning, we know that this movement represents a revolt against the present state of Western man. It therefore enters within the perspectives of my researches, and I shall have to come back to it at a later time.

While waiting for a fuller study, I would like to note this: all my analyses deal with human groups characterized by and submitted to a particular oppression—the black Americans are a minority group within a total society which treats them in a certain way; the colonized are a people, though a majority in their land, who are in fact dominated by a more powerful people. The phenomenon with which we are faced today may seem completely new, and it pleases us to dwell on this absolute novelty. It is no longer a matter of the domination of one group of men by another group of men, but of the alienation of modern man in general, of the man of industrial civilization, soon followed by all mankind, for that seems to be the general destiny.

Arguments are not lacking for such a thesis. Contemporary society seems irresistibly pulled towards total productivity; the laws of this maximum productivity demand that individuals be first of all sacrificed to it before receiving its benefits. This sickness reaches the socialist countries as well, countries in which

profit is not the motivation of the entrepreneurs. The phenomenon is a general one, since its rises above classes, peoples and
nations and perhaps—though no one has dared say it—the
dominating and the dominated.

I must, however, merely recall that this way of considering
the misfortune of humanity as a whole is not as novel as it
may appear. I don't say it is totally false or useless. For my
part, I have shown that the colonizer *also* pays the price for
colonization, and the white American, I am convinced, will not
emerge unscathed from his confrontation with the problem of
the blacks. In a word, there exists an alienation of the oppressor
as well. Nonetheless, I would like to see it admitted that the
class struggle does not explain everything. I have already challenged this formula as an explanation for colonization or anti-
Semitism; I feel too that it is completely inadequate to explain
the condition of women. In the end, it is not impossible that
the struggle against a ceaselessly recurring alienation is one of
the moral imperatives of all societies.

However, does this alienation common to all men, this permanent misfortune, eclipse the various specific misfortunes, the
particular oppressions from which each human group suffers?
I don't believe so at all. And I must state clearly that if this
view, whether new or not, of the events through which we are
living should lead to the obscuring of these different oppressions, I would then fear a new hoax and a new attitude of resignation. Since the misfortune is a general one and we are all
affected by it—rich and poor, black and white, the free and the
dependent, men and women—then what good is it to fight
against an evil which is almost basic?

I ask, on the contrary, if it wouldn't be more appropriate
even there to proceed to differential analyses. Not everyone
suffers from the failures of industrial civilization in the same
way and to the same extent. If the colonizer pays his tribute to
the colonial relationship, he still derives from it more advantages than disadvantages. And though the privileged of our so-

cieties are, to some extent, alienated by the system, they do profit from it on the whole. Even in the midst of industrial civilization, finally, the question remains: who is actually oppressed, and to the advantage of whom?

This inequality in the common misfortune—if there is a common misfortune—is not of purely theoretical interest. It has considerable practical consequences. It would be naïve, for example, to believe that it is enough to point out the fundamental evils of industrialization in order to make men aware of and obtain their help against oppression. The health of the oppressed can only come from the oppressed themselves, even in an industrial society. This is, in any case, the only way to have an effective grip on the social destiny of all men. All else, no matter how seductive for the philosophic spirit, risks to be nothing but another way, hardly new, of begging the question.